"Julie does an excellent job of shining a light on the safety issues facing our kids today. Her vision for child safety begins with a Christian worldview, is full of biblical wisdom, and encourages parents to trust God with their kids. This is a great resource for parents seeking to equip their kids to follow Christ in a fallen world."

> **Jeff Dalrymple,** Executive Director, Evangelical Council for Abuse Prevention (ECAP)

"Julie Lowe's *Safeguards* is a must-read for parents. Full of practical wisdom and grounded in biblical principles, this book trains parents to identify potential dangers and proactively equip their kids. We expect to return to these principles again and again in our own home. Highly recommend!"

> **Deepak and Sara Reju,** Capitol Hill Baptist Church, Washington, DC; author of *On Guard* (Deepak) and *Jesus Saves* (Sara)

"When a parenting question comes up that my husband and I are wrestling with, he says, 'Can you ask Julie?' As a colleague of Julie's, I do go and ask her! With this book, now all parents have access to Julie—access to her wisdom, her decades of experience, and her deep heart for the well-being of children. Parents, this book will equip you to be both proactive and helpfully responsive to so many of the challenges that arise in parenting. I need this book, and I trust you will find you need it too as you dig in!"

> **Lauren Whitman,** Faculty and counselor, CCEF; developmental editor, *Journal of Biblical Counseling*

"This is such an important and timely book. Though geared toward parents, this book is important for counselors, pastors, teachers, and youth leaders to read as well. Julie is unafraid to approach topics that many are hesitant to address, such as sexual abuse, pornography, sexting, and mental health, and she does so with a strong Scriptural base. She doesn't merely encourage parental involvement but gives practical steps for involvement without being simplistic or formulaic."

> **David and Krista Dunham,** Biblical Counselors, Cornerstone Community Soul Care, Metro Detroit; authors of *Table for Two: Biblical Counsel for Eating Disorders*

"Children and teens face many situations where they need discernment to make wise choices and stay safe. Julie Lowe's vast experience shines in *Safeguards: Shielding Our Homes and Equipping Our Kids.* She provides biblical principles and practical guidelines that help you impart invaluable wisdom to your children. Every parent navigating the challenges of our modern world needs this book!"

Darby Strickland, Faculty and counselor, CCEF; author of *Is it Abuse?*

"*Safeguards* could not possibly be more practical. Every page is loaded with applied wisdom for keeping children safe. I constantly found myself saying 'Our family needs to do this!' Grounded in a call to trust the Lord rather than fearmongering, *Safeguards* equips both children and parents to discern evil and danger and to prepare wise, protective responses."

Alasdair Groves, Executive Director, CCEF

"In Julie Lowe's latest book, readers will once again benefit from her sound biblical theology, counselor's heart, and years of experience walking alongside parents and children in a broken and unsafe world. This book is not intended to produce fear and anxiety for parents (we have enough of that already) but to provide wise, winsome, and practical guidance to help your child navigate a broken world with the hope of Jesus Christ."

Jonathan D. Holmes, Executive Director, Fieldstone Counseling

"Reading this book is like gaining a wise mentor to walk alongside you in your parenting journey. Julie Lowe expertly tackles key challenges parents face and provides scripts, scenarios, principles, and guidelines that are steeped with biblical wisdom. If you are looking to equip your children for the potential dangers and difficulties they may face in life, consider this your handbook."

Eliza Huie, Licensed and biblical counselor; Director of Counseling, McLean Bible Church, Vienna, VA; coauthor of *The Whole Life*

"The most common response from parents who read *Safeguards* will be, 'Finally! A parenting book that doesn't just discuss discipline strategies.' Julie provides biblical principles and sample conversations for everything from technology, dating, mental health, abuse prevention, and sleepovers. Get it, read it, and you'll reference it time and again over the years as these topics emerge in your home."

Brad Hambrick, Pastor of Counseling, The Summit Church, Durham, NC; author of *Making Sense of Forgiveness*

SAFEGUARDS

SHIELDING OUR HOMES AND EQUIPPING OUR KIDS

Julie Lowe

New
Growth
Press

newgrowthpress.com

New Growth Press, Greensboro, NC 27401
newgrowthpress.com
Copyright © 2022 by Julie Lowe

Cover Design: Faceout Studios, faceoutstudio.com
Interior Design and Typesetting: Gretchen Logterman

ISBN: 978-1-64507-286-7 (Print)
ISBN: 978-1-64507-287-4 (eBook)

Library of Congress Cataloging-in-Publication Data on file

Printed in the United States of America

29 28 27 26 25 24 23 22   1 2 3 4 5

Contents

Foreword

It was not my best or brightest moment. Luella, my dear wife, was the safety marshal in the family. One night as we were finishing dinner, she said, "I want to talk about what we would do if our house caught on fire. Paul, you start." Without a moment's thought I said, "I'd grab my guitar and get it out of the house!" Luella looked at me rather shocked and said, "What about us?" As I sat there mortified at the revelation of my selfish materialism, my kids laughed and said, "Yep, gotta save that guitar, Dad."

Luella was right—safety skills are essential this side of eternity, and as I demonstrated, we are not always prepared to make wise choices. And here is the burden that every parent carries: you are tasked by God to be his primary tool for the formation of the souls that he has placed in your care. These souls have physical bodies that must be nurtured and protected as well.

The best word for the role of a parent is *ambassador*. An ambassador represents the one who sent him or her. Parenting is not first about what we want for our children or what we want from our children, but what God has for them and requires from them. In everything you do, in all the little moments as a parent, you are representing the one who sent you.

God makes his invisible authority visible by sending parents to oversee their children. God makes his invisible wisdom visible in the lives of children by sending parents to impart his wisdom to them. God makes his invisible guardianship visible by sending parents to children who need to be guarded and protected. There is no achievement, no hunt for success, no busyness of life, no hope or dream, no craving of the heart that should ever get in the way of our daily calling to be God's ambassador in the lives of those he has placed in our care.

Being an ambassador means there are some settled beliefs that should daily motivate you. These beliefs are trustworthy because they are rooted in the truths of God's Word, and they are vital because they give you practical tracks to run on. First and foremost, parents must be deeply persuaded that *God is wise and good*. God is the ultimate and glorious definition of everything that is wise and good. This means it is impossible for him to direct us to do anything that would be bad for us. And because he is glorious in grace, he unleashes his wisdom, goodness, sovereignty, and power for the ultimate good of his children.

Second, it is vital to not minimize that you parent your children in a *deeply broken world* that does not function as God originally intended. For his glory and our good, God has chosen for this groaning, dysfunctional world to be our present address. It is biblical to say that this world is not safe, but we must also say we are being guarded and protected by our heavenly Father for a world that will someday be free of evil, danger, sin, and suffering forever and ever. Being God's ambassador in the lives of your children means never minimizing the dangers of life in this sin-broken world.

Third, it is important for parents to understand that because God's ways are always right and because there is evil all around in this fallen world, the *wisdom of discernment is a vital commitment and skill.* Discernment is the ability to apply God's wisdom to the specific choices that face you in this broken world. It is the skill of knowing right from wrong, safety from danger, and good from evil. Children aren't naturally discerning; in fact, the Bible tells us that they are born with foolishness in their hearts. So, a practical commitment to teaching conceptual and functional discernment to our children is essential.

What I have written so far is why I love *Safeguards.* I know of no other book that does what this one does. Here is practical help for every parent who is preparing their children to live with discernment in our sadly broken world. Read and absorb its wisdom—you will gain so much insight here and loads of practical skills to pass down to your children. But perhaps the thing that I love the most about this book is that its practical focus isn't separated from the beauty and comfort of the gospel of Jesus Christ. Julie reminds us again and again of God's presence, goodness, and grace. She comforts us with the truth that he cares for our children more than we ever will. And she assures us that there is no wisdom so wise as the wisdom of the Lord. What you are about to read will change your life as a parent and will help you prepare your children to live with discernment both now and when they are no longer under your care.

Paul David Tripp

Introduction:
The Need to Equip Our Kids

For over twenty years I have worked with numerous churches, ministries, and families when the children under their care experienced abuse and mistreatment. I have met with many parents who ask heart-wrenching questions. They wonder how their child could have gotten caught up in online bullying, sexting, pornography, or grooming by a pedophile.

Parents and caregivers whose children have been victimized or hurt in some way struggle to understand how such grievous wrongs occurred. Was there something they could have done to prevent it? Did they miss warning signs? Are they responsible for their child's struggles? It is distressing to evaluate in hindsight.

Those questions are then followed up with: What can we do now? How can we help our child now? How can we prevent this in the future? The alarming statistics related to child sexual abuse, online predation, severe bullying by peers, and more lead thoughtful parents to ask: How do we protect children and young people from such things happening? How do we proactively put in place safeguards to protect our children from the dangers of this world?

I didn't write this book to scare you. As a counselor I do walk with many families through some of the worst cases that I hope you will never have to face. At the same time, God calls parents to protect and equip their children, who are born weak and vulnerable. I wrote this book to assist you in that task by applying biblical principles that result in common sense and practical strategies that will help safeguard your children so they can thrive.

Foundational Principles for Understanding This Book

The foundation for all that is written in this book is threefold. First, we live in a broken, fallen world. There is danger and evil, sickness and disease, corruption, deception, and temptation. We cannot live in this world without seeing the effects of it on our lives and the lives of our children.

Consider these passages from Scripture:

We know that we are from God, and the whole world lies in the power of the evil one. (1 John 5:19)

Evil people and impostors will go on from bad to worse, deceiving and being deceived. (2 Timothy 3:13)

A troublemaker and a villain, who goes about with a corrupt mouth, who winks maliciously with his eye, signals with his feet and motions with fingers, who plots evil with deceit in his heart . . . (Proverbs 6:12–14 NIV)

And this is the judgment: the light has come into the world, and people loved the darkness rather than the light because their works were evil. (John 3:19)

Therefore just as sin came into the world through one man, and death through sin, and so death spread to all men because all sinned. (Romans 5:12)

Dangerous people prowl upon the weak and naive. Evil is cunning; it deceives and entices. It promises pleasure but delivers brokenness. Evil is both done to us and seduces us from within. Accepting this reality means that we must raise children who can navigate and respond to potential dangers.

Scripture is full of wisdom on how to respond. Matthew 10:16 tells us, "Behold, I am sending you out like sheep in the midst of wolves; so be wise as serpents and innocent as doves." Proverbs 27:12 advises, "The prudent sees danger and hides himself, but the simple go on and suffer for it." Proverbs goes on to reiterate, "One who is wise is cautious and turns from evil, but a fool is reckless and careless" (Proverbs 14:16).

The Bible teaches us that wise people see the potential for danger and take measures to protect themselves. Wise people are cautious and discerning, and turn from evil. Those who do not act with such wisdom are called naive, simple, and foolish, and they suffer for it. Clearly, there is nothing good that comes from being unaware of the danger that exists in our world. Too often parents are unwilling to face the realities of the perils that exist in the world around us, and therefore conceal such realities from their children. But if we only shelter our children and do not equip them to act in wisdom, we inadvertently raise naive, simple children who do not know how to make sense of evil and wisely navigate it.

Second, we teach our children to navigate this world by giving them the ability to discern good from evil and right from wrong. Our culture is pressing in on our children, indoctrinating them with false views of romance and love, morality and truth, sexuality and identity. Our world calls intolerant what is good and holy, and calls good what God calls wicked. Isaiah 5:20 says, "Woe to those who call evil good and good evil, who put darkness for light and light for darkness, who put bitter for sweet and sweet for bitter!"

Keeping our children safe means we teach them God's ways—how he created us to live following him. Safety is built on the foundation of discerning right from wrong. Our children cannot safely navigate this world without the ability to distinguish good from evil. As a parent, my ultimate goal for my children is not to keep them safe (though it is *a* goal); rather, it is that my children would know the ways of God and walk in truth. Walking by faith and knowing good from evil will be their shield, and I believe that safety skills will be the fruit of teaching our children the ways of the Lord.

Teaching our children good from evil will produce in them both wisdom and discernment. As I hope you will see throughout the course of this book, wisdom and discernment are the substance of what I hope you (and your children) learn from this resource. Consider this verse: "But solid food is for the mature, for those who have their powers of discernment trained by constant practice to distinguish good from evil" (Hebrews 5:14). Notice that the mature have *"powers of discernment,"* trained by *"constant practice to distinguish good from evil."*

Discussing the dangers our children might encounter helps us to understand how we can begin the process of equipping both ourselves and our children for setting up appropriate protective measures. This book is about naming the darkness existing in this world and equipping our children to know how to avoid it and respond to it if it finds them. Doing so also protects our young people from the temptations around them and the entanglements of destructive choices.

Throughout the book I emphasize role-playing and discussion in order to practice discernment, evaluating right from wrong. At times when I talk about safety skills, the goals of discernment and wisdom will be explicit, and other times it will be implicit, but it will always be the substance of what I hope to accomplish.

Philippians 1:9–10 affirms this goal: "And it is my prayer that your love may abound more and more, with knowledge and all discernment, so that you may approve what is excellent, and so be pure and blameless for the day of Christ." We are to commit ourselves to train, disciple, educate, and equip our kids so that they can be given the myriad of tools they need to wisely navigate this world while walking in fellowship with the Lord.

Knowing good from evil, right from wrong is primary; safety skills are secondary. Safety skills are a fruit of the way we parent our children. This is important to emphasize, because if we raise children who somehow have been shielded from the worst perils of this world but do not walk with the Lord, do not know right from wrong, or are unaware of the dangers that exist from within—we have failed them miserably.

The third foundation for this book is the understanding that our safety ultimately rests in the hands of our God. Psalm 37:39–40 reminds us, "The salvation of the righteous is from the Lord; he is their stronghold in time of trouble. The Lord helps them and delivers them, he delivers them from the wicked and saves them, because they take refuge in him." Our ultimate hope is in a sovereign God who is our high tower, our very present help in trouble (Psalm 46:1; Proverbs 18:10). Consider the following passages:

> Though I walk in the midst of trouble, you preserve my life; you stretch out your hand against the wrath of my enemies, and your right hand delivers me. (Psalm 138:7)

> But the LORD is faithful. He will establish you and guard you against the evil one. (2 Thessalonians 3:3)

> The fear of man lays a snare, but whoever trusts in the LORD is safe. (Proverbs 29:25)

Psalm 23 is a profound reminder that we will walk through dark valleys, we will face enemies, we will come face-to-face with evil, and he will be our Shepherd, guiding us and walking with us in the difficult places. His presence is our comfort, our hope, and our very present help.

I've written a whole book on teaching our kids safety, but at the end of the day, God is the one who watches over us. Ultimately, this is a book about teaching kids to live in the light and navigate the darkness of this world while in a trusting relationship with their loving, heavenly Father. As we explore Scripture, we will understand more deeply the call to be wise, to see danger and run from it (Proverbs 27:12), to have courage (2 Chronicles 32:7–9; Proverbs 28:1), and to stand up for those who cannot stand up for themselves (Proverbs 31:8–9; Isaiah 1:17). We are not to be passive in our engagement with injustice, danger, mistreatment, and evil. We must respond to it, while resting in our ultimate Protector.

Why Safeguards?

What do I mean when I use the term "safeguards?" It means working with you to establish a home and a worldview that protects your children. Parents are the first line of defense. We are tasked with the care, protection, and discipling of our children. We must discern immediate and future danger and have a plan for how to combat it. We are the primary educators of our children. Our job is to give them the knowledge and skills to navigate the world around them. Yet, when it comes to sexual predators, online dangers, bullying, and other common dangers, parents are often silent because they don't know what to do or don't know where to start.

Our children will be faced with risks and hazards, and it is our job to teach and prepare them. They will also find themselves (like us) tempted by things that threaten to undo them. A biblical worldview understands that we must not only guard against the dangers and perils around us; we must guard our own hearts from corruption.

For some of you, this book will be a welcome resource. You have long been aware of the dangers that exist. You are acutely aware of the need to both protect and equip young people. Maybe you experienced some of these hazards in your own life and you wish to save your children from similar grief. Perhaps you've seen firsthand in the life of your child, relative, or friend, how such harmful things can unfold. You are aware and on board. You can now be part of prevention by being equipped and helping equip those around you.

For some others, this may feel like a shock to your system. Perhaps you think, "Surely it is not this bad," or "She is overreacting and planting fear in us." I assure you I am not. As both a parent and a counselor, I have seen and heard too many stories to count. Stories of children and teens, from families like mine and like yours, being exposed to the evils of this world and seeing the wake of destruction it leaves. Accepting this helps us to become wiser in response.

I can assure you I have no desire for you to live in fear or anxiety. A door of danger has not suddenly opened before you; the door was always open. Your children are vulnerable. The difficulty is that many parents believe ignorance is bliss. Parents say to me, "The less I know, the better. I don't think I want to know what my kids are doing on social media." Do we actually believe it is better to be unaware while our children open the door and face threats regularly? We must choose to live with eyes wide open.

My goal is to equip you and your children. This book is about safety as the fruit of distinguishing good from evil, of developing discernment and wisdom. The Lord says he gives it generously to those who ask (James 1:5). We are entreated to not be caught off guard by the entrapments and perils of this world. We are to be wise, discerning people. We are to safeguard our homes, equip our children, and trust the One who is our refuge. When we do this, we are able to lay our heads down at night because the Lord is, and will be, our safety. When we have done all that we can to safeguard our homes, then we can be like David, and even in the face of danger say, "In peace I will both lie down and sleep; for you alone, O LORD, make me dwell in safety" (Psalm 4:8). Our heavenly Father is our true safeguard and we can trust him.

Part One

WISDOM—THE FOUNDATION FOR EQUIPPING CHILDREN WITH SAFETY SKILLS

CHAPTER 1

Unique Dangers in Our Modern World

"I do not ask that you take them out of the world, but that you keep them from the evil one." John 17:15

All it takes is less than an hour of watching the local news to become aware of the dangers that our children confront every day as they go out into the world. Consider some of these common risks to young people:

- Rising reports of youth depression, suicide, and anxiety[1]
- Marijuana and drug use becoming more common place
- Bullying and cyberbullying increasing with technology[2]
- Young and younger children being exposed to pornography, sexting, and solicitation[3]
- Sexual activity, orientation, and identity issues on the rise
- Internet and online addiction
- A growing culture of violence, objectification, and desensitization of the mistreatment of others
- Physical abuse, sexual abuse, date rape, and trafficking of young people
- School shootings, teens encouraging other teens to commit self-harm, and dangerous viral social media challenges

This chapter will give you a bird's eye overview of some of the unique dangers that children face today. As the saying goes, "forewarned is forearmed." Before we discuss how to equip our children with the safety skills they need to thrive in our world, we have to face squarely the threats that they might encounter.

Technology

With the entrance of social media and personal electronic devices, a world of new possibilities—carrying with it both blessings and dangers—have poured into our children's lives. Children and teens are being given devices with little preparation on how to steward them. These shiny objects (smartphones, tablets, smart watches, and the like) are handed to your son or daughter, opening a world of entertainment and connectivity. Unless precise parental controls have been activated, children and teenagers have access to a plethora of online games and apps, they can text and video with anyone they wish, they have access to video streaming services, social media, and a wealth of information via internet browsers, and all of it is promptly available at their fingertips.

On the positive side, kids can get help with their homework, find out how to build anything from a fort to a chicken coop, learn a second language, and listen to podcasts, sermons, music, and stories. They can connect with others who share their hobbies and interests, or with kids of a like-minded community who feel different or have disabilities.

But many hazards are also present. Pornography sites target young people by researching commonly misspelled words and redirecting youth to porn sites and images they will be tempted to click on. Online games have people trolling and making connections with children, hoping to gather personal information, gain access to a child's world, or lure young people away from home and into all kinds of horrid lifestyles. Romans 16:17–18 warns us that " . . . such persons do not serve our Lord Christ, but their own appetites, and by smooth talk and flattery they deceive the hearts of the naive." Our young people are actively being pursued by evil influences. Videos, chat rooms, and cultural influencers all win a voice in your child's life that is often louder, more consistent, and more accessible than ours.

As a counselor, I hear young people regularly report unwanted sexual solicitations, online provocation, unsolicited exposure to "sexting," and sexual material. We have handed over a small device with a world of good and evil. As parents and caregivers, we need to consider the hazards and ask ourselves if our children are mature and responsible enough to handle them. If we answer yes, then we need to teach them to steward such privileges and put accountability in place to shepherd them.

The Influence of Peers

Peer pressure and influence is not a new thing. We can trace it back to Adam and Eve as they listened to the voice of evil pressuring them to not believe that God is good and for them. As the apostle Paul said, "Do not be deceived: 'Bad company ruins good morals.'" (1 Corinthians 15:33). It's easy to understand that all of us are shaped by those around us. But our children are especially vulnerable to being influenced by the views of their peers. Their voices are loud, compelling, and promise affirmation, freedom, and acceptance. Such voices seduce kids to believe that something good is being withheld from them and that they must pursue it on their own.

In the modern world, as children get older, they begin to ask questions related to their worldview and identity, and they want to know if what they have been taught is true. Preteens and teens often struggle to accept that their parents have the best answers about relationships, identity, activities, and even questions of meaning and purpose. They are drawn to the most persistent voices in their lives (their peers) to help answer these questions. The desire to fit in and please becomes dangerously strong. This means that it matters who speaks into their lives. What kinds of friends are they choosing? Who are they spending large amounts of time with? Proverb says, "Whoever walks with the wise becomes wise, but the companion of fools will suffer harm" (Proverbs 13:20).

Of equal concern is the progressive eradication of positive, mature, adult influences in the lives of older children and teens. Young people are parenting and shaping each other. They are in school together, they are in extracurricular activities together, and they are online together, on social media together, gaming together, texting together. They are rarely disconnected from their peer group. As a result, they are becoming their own source of wisdom.

Access to smartphones, social media, and the internet, means that peer influence press in more and more; it also means that parents struggle more and more to have a voice in their children's lives. Most parents want to be intentionally influencing and shaping their child's character, but that requires a significant investment of time and thought. If parents are not actively building relationships and educating their children, someone (or something) else will shape them. When mature, godly influences are removed, or at least diminished, young people will be guided by their friends and culture. When we—quite literally— leave our young people to their own devices, they will look for guidance from their peers and "disciple" one another in these ways:

- A false sense of maturity/confidence in their self-knowledge
- An inability to occupy themselves or be alone
- Proneness to alienate from adult influence
- Tolerance for bad behavior and inappropriate peer demands
- Intolerance of wisdom and a mockery of what is good and wholesome
- Turning a blind eye to immoral and risky behavior
- Disparaging authority as irrelevant

Indeed, the companion of fools will suffer harm, but when our kids walk with the wise, they will become wise (Proverbs 13:20). Loving adult influence will help children in these ways:

- Build respect and cooperation
- Create an atmosphere of deference and admiration

- Provide security for children
- Encourage a child's healthy dependence on parents and adults for spiritual and emotional nurturing
- Model a reliance on wise counsel, especially from the Lord
- Display a proper respect for leadership and authority

Paul, in his letter to Titus talks at length about the need for Christians to influence a younger generation in what is right and good. We are called to model saying "No" to ungodliness and worldly passions, and to live self-controlled, upright, and godly lives in this present age (Titus 2:12). We live in a world that can turn everything that is right and good upside down for kids. What is good is called evil, and what is evil is called good. If we do not talk with, listen to, nurture, and walk alongside our kids, they will be drawn into the value system surrounding them.

Culture

We live in a world that is distinctly self-oriented. Consider these cultural clichés: "Look out for number one;" "You do you;" "The greatest love of all is self-love;" "Do what's right for you;" "Live your truth." The list can go on and on. Our kids are inundated with a version of moral relativism that seeks to sweep them away with the current of their peers. It is the cultural air they breathe. It is the environment they are educated in, and it is the constant beat of the media drum.

These messages lead our kids to question what is right and good. Their surrounding culture can easily shape their values and ideas regarding moral absolutes, relationships, romance, sexuality, identity, and how or what informs their decision-making. A secular culture will sway your children to embrace a worldview devoid of God, and they can quickly be swept away by the ideology and behaviors that go with it.

When these messages are internalized, young people often decide that the highest good is what they personally choose as good. It leads to looking out for themselves, sometimes at the expense of stepping on others. Or they swing to meaninglessness, despair, lack of motivation, and a downward spiral to depression or suicide.

Along with holding out to our children the value of self-love and self-orientation, the world puts doubt in their minds about God's Word. Scripture and its authority are under attack. We ourselves may even attempt to reinterpret God's Word to fit our beliefs and choices. When our children begin to doubt what God says, and to question his care for us, they start to move toward what feels right to them. Their desire for autonomy becomes more powerful and informative than God's Word.

Truth has become subjective—that's why people so easily talk about "my truth." This leads to the breakdown of any moral absolutes and the rise of individual sovereignty. Our kids learn to chase after things that promise to deliver joy, pleasure, fulfillment, connection, and identity, but they lead to death. Ultimately, there is a battle in our children's hearts and minds between revealed truth and subjective truth.

It is sobering how it only takes a generation to lose sight of God's ways. The need for parents to safeguard their children from empty philosophies is greater than ever. Judges 2:10 says: "And all that generation also were gathered to their fathers. And there arose another generation after them who did not know the LORD or the work that he had done for Israel."

"Change is always one generation away," the atheist Bill Hallowell said. "So if we can plant seeds of doubt in our children, religion will go away in a generation, or at least largely go away—that's what I think we have an obligation to do."[4] Make no mistake about it, our generation and the generations to follow are actively being proselytized, persuaded, and converted to a new relative truth.

Secular thought says we are most human when we are in charge of ourselves. Christian thought says the opposite—we are most human when we give up control and trust a sovereign God with ourselves. How the world around us thinks can be compelling, but Paul reminds us, "See to it that no one takes you captive by philosophy and empty deceit, according to human tradition, according to the elemental spirits of the world, and not according to Christ" (Colossians 2:8).

The Danger Also Lies Within

"The good person out of the good treasure of his heart produces good, and the evil person out of the evil treasure produces evil, for out of the abundance of the heart his mouth speaks" (Luke 6:45).

You can and should maintain a close watch on your children. You can and should monitor their activities and try to shelter them from harm. But you will find that the danger your children face cannot always be kept at bay. We must equip them to function wisely in the world and to know good from evil. Good parenting is not simply about putting up boundaries and high walls—protecting our children from the external dangers of this world. Wise parenting also helps children understand that there is also danger from within. Sin resides in the heart and is not easily visible. Every person—loved ones, trusted friends and acquaintances, respectable individuals with whom we live and work—is capable of being led astray into destructive choices. This includes your own children.

In 2004, M. Night Shyamalan produced the movie *The Village*. It is a story of a group of adults who, after experiencing their own victimization and suffering, decided to withdraw from the outside world in order to protect themselves and their families from future harm. A village was created, and it was purposely surrounded by a forest filled with evil creatures, which kept their villagers contained and "safe" from the outside world.

In a desire to escape the tragedy and evils of the outside world, they created their own protected environment, believing the lie that evil exists "out there" beyond themselves. They quickly find out the evil they sought to avoid exists within the very walls they built. Indeed, it existed within them. Being ill-equipped for this reality led to devastating consequences.

Aleksandr Solzhenitsyn, in *The Gulag Archipelago*, says it like this: "The line separating good and evil passes not through states,

15

nor between classes, nor between political parties either—but right through every human heart—and through all human hearts."[5]

Jesus tells us, "For from within, out of the heart of man, come evil thoughts, sexual immorality, theft, murder, adultery, coveting, wickedness, deceit, sensuality, envy, slander, pride, foolishness" (Mark 7:21–22). Yes, each of us is vulnerable to evil happening to us, but we are also each capable of allowing it to take root *in* us. Our children need to be taught to guard their hearts, for it is the wellspring of life (Proverbs 4:23). James reminds us about the slippery slope of giving in to sinful desires: " . . . desire when it has conceived gives birth to sin, and sin when it is fully grown brings forth death" (James 1:15). We will fail our children if we only shelter them from the external perils of this world and do not foster in them a conviction to guard themselves from corruption.

We can try to keep evil far from us, but we will fail because of the pervasive nature of sin and evil. Your children will be tempted by their own wrong desires. Just like you, they will sometimes fall. They will sometimes go in the wrong direction. But this is the very issue that the gospel of Jesus Christ addresses. Jesus died on a cruel cross because we are all sinners. On that cross, all of our sins were forgiven—the sins of parents and children alike. Isaiah 53:6 says: "All we like sheep have gone astray; we have turned—every one—to his own way; and the LORD has laid on him the iniquity of us all." We have been rescued from ourselves—and continue to be. We and our families have been given a Helper and Comforter who transforms hearts and minds—places that no one else can go.

Our ultimate safety, and our children's safety, will be found in trusting a faithful Father who has rescued us and continues to rescue us. Even as we spend the rest of the book discussing how to protect our children from the dangers in this world, remember the good news that you have to share with your children—that Jesus Christ came to save sinners (1 Timothy 1:15). Then together you can remember that "He who is in you is greater than he who is in the world" (1 John 4:4).

The Challenge: How to Be Salt and Light

Knowing that Jesus is more powerful than the deluge of pressures and risks facing our kids is a great starting point, but it can still be hard to know what would be a uniquely Christian response to the dangers our children are exposed to. Should we remove our children from society and all technological devices, seeking to have complete control over every influence that may come their way? Is that what it means to protect our kids?

Jesus points the way forward for us by using the metaphors of salt and light to illustrate how his followers are to live in the world (Matthew 5:13–16). We are to preserve and illuminate what is good, both before our children and our communities. We must enhance the broken world around us. Our lives as redeemed children of God should have an obvious heartening affect to those with whom we work and live. This is the posture we want to pass on to our kids. Instead of being terrified of the dangers our children face, or sticking our head in the proverbial sand and pretending they don't exist, we can turn to Christ for the help we need to teach and equip our children to be both salt and light.

But it does take careful thinking to figure out what it looks like to be "in the world but not of the world" (John 17:14–19). Scripture tells us to not be conformed to this world (Romans 12:2) and to be renewed in our minds (Ephesians 4:23), but it also teaches us that Jesus didn't pray that we would be taken out of this world, but that we would be kept from the evil one (John 17:15).

When we faithfully image Christ to the world around us, we illuminate the path for them to their Creator. We want to raise our children and equip them in such a way that when the world sees their lives, they are drawn to Christ and his ways.

Our faithfulness should be evident to all. The behavior of God's people should be a light that draws others to it. We need to remember that salt must not lose its flavor and light must not be concealed or dimmed. It is tempting to look at all the hard things we will be discussing and believe the darkness is too great, but we must "not be overcome by evil, but overcome evil with good (Romans 12:21).

How do we equip our children to live in their world and as salt and light? Their character must be shaped and transformed by a personal relationship with Christ. We instill a love for the Lord and for all that is right and good and holy. We point them to what Scripture tells us: "For we are his workmanship, created in Christ Jesus for good works, which God prepared beforehand, that we should walk in them" (Galatians 2:10). Young people will become salt and light when they learn to walk with the Lord.

Our children's greatest defense against the evil of this world will be to know God and his ways. Then they will know the straight path to take and will be able to recognize the crooked path and avoid it. You and I should have no greater joy than that our children walk in truth (3 John 1:4). As a parent, do not grow weary discipling your children; the Lord and his Spirit will be your help. Take encouragement for your journey from 2 Corinthians 9:8: "And God is able to make all grace abound to you, so having the sufficiency in all things at all times, you may abound in every good work."

CHAPTER 2

Worry and Denial Are
Not Safety Skills

"Can any one of you by worrying add a single hour to your life?"
Matthew 6:27 (NIV)

When it comes to addressing and responding to safety issues regarding our children, there are many common struggles parents face. Instead of facing reality head on with an appropriate dose of both realism and faith, it is easy to veer off course in the diverging directions of either fear or denial. Neither response will enable you to make healthy decisions or appropriately equip your children for the challenges they will face. Neither response will enable you to grow in love and dependence on the Lord, nor help your child to do so. Let's dig into each struggle and see the better way Christ offers us.

Fear and Worry—Not Useful Safety Skills

Parents worry about germs, cancer, choking, kidnapping, drugs and alcohol, school performance and academics, and many other things—the list is endless for all of us. But worrying is not a tactic that will keep our kids safe. Our anxiety does nothing but take up time and mental energy.

I've heard many parents refer to themselves as worriers. Some parents wear their worry like a badge of honor. For them it almost seems like their worrying proves they love their children and that somehow it keeps their children safe.

But does worry increase safety? The short, but surprising answer: It does not. What worry does do is blur your ability to see genuine threats clearly. Worry is about all the what ifs, the possibilities, and your own insecurities and fears of the future. It distracts you from living in the present and perceiving what is going on in front of you. It hinders wisdom and discernment.

Gavin de Becker writes in his book *Protecting the Gift*, "Perception and not worry is what serves safety. Perception focuses your attention; worry blurs it."[6]

Time and again, we think if we put enough focused concern into all the possible dangers our children might face, then perhaps, we can will them out of existence. We believe that such hyper-attention will produce some benefits. Instead, worry puts us in a state of being perpetually fearful. In that state, we cannot discern what is truly a threat or what might be harmless. For the anxious parent, everything feels like a threat.

Worry prevents us from living fully in the present. It makes our children hesitant to take risks, experience the resiliency of failure and success, and hinders them from experiencing new things. Parents who worry try to control their world, frequently shrinking it to whatever size feels manageable. The result is that they unintentionally prevent their children from living life fully. Children who grow up with anxious parents often feel suffocated.

Worry is crippling to both a parent and a child's sense of safety and stability. A parent who chronically worries will most likely raise a child who worries. Children who worry are not adept at handling challenges; rather, they struggle to take risk, try new things, and interact with people. By worrying, instead of preventing harm, we can actually cause harm in our children.

It is not by accident that Scripture says, "Fear not" over 365 times. The Bible is not implying danger does not exist. Nor is it implying you will never have hard things happen to you or your children. As a matter of fact, we see over and over again that the Bible tells us to not be surprised by trials and tribulation, by suffering and evil—it does exist (John 16:33; James 1:2–8; 1 Peter 4:12; 1 Peter 5:10).

Worry also presumes a functionally godless existence. Simply put, worry tells us that God must not be present or in control, therefore, I must figure out how to keep my children safe. But in the midst of trouble, God reminds us again and again that he is our refuge and a very present help in trouble (Psalm 46:1–3). Worry says, "I must figure out and control my world." Faith says, "God is in control and will equip me (or my child) with wisdom for the moment."

As my former colleague and CCEF (Christian Counseling & Education Foundation) executive director, the late David Powlison, often talked about, in this life we may have many reasons to be afraid, but we have even better reasons not to fear, when we consider who the Lord is and how he's on our side.[7] What a comforting thought when we are tempted to be paralyzed by mountains of "what ifs!"

There will be plenty to fear in this world, but we cannot be ruled by it. As believers, we know that there is a God who is sovereign over all. He is our help, refuge, and wisdom, and a sure comfort in the hard places and times. Joshua 1:9 reminds us, "Have not I commanded you? Be strong and courageous. Do not be frightened, and do not be dismayed, for the LORD your God is with you wherever you go." In any difficult situation, we are called to trust God, but also to take steps of faith and courage. In the face of all the dangers our children might be exposed to, we trust God to be with us and we trust God to help us be wise, practice discernment, and guard our homes. Then we put our hope in him.

Denial—Also Not a Useful Safety Skill

When faced with the threats our children may be exposed to, the opposite struggle for parents is denial. Some parents take pride in not struggling with worry or fear as other parents do. They watch from a window while their young children play outside with their neighbor friend. They are jumping off rocks, running in and out of the house, and climbing trees in the woods. They are confident that their children are happy and safe.

However, they might be oblivious to the older teenager who is also watching them from his window. This teen struggles with pornography and has begun looking for ways to act out the sexual fantasies he has been watching. He sees his little brother playing with kids, watches them running in and out of the house passed him. He considers ways to entice one of the children into his room, the bathroom, or the basement while the other kids are distracted. He plans to bribe them with a movie or video game and isolate them so he can molest each one.

Perhaps if someone were to tell you that such a possibility exists, you'd brush them off, call them an alarmist, or shake your head in disbelief. Denial ignores possibilities and refuses to accept such things as an option in their neighborhood, community, home, or family. Denial rationalizes, minimizes, and explains away genuine concerns or red flags.

In a desire to avoid discomfort, or perhaps because we absolutely have no idea how to approach such matters, we tell ourselves our children could never be sexually abused. We assure ourselves that we can keep our kids safe, that we know our neighbors and friends. Or perhaps you choose to believe you can protect your kids by keeping them at home where evil cannot touch them. You are unaware that as they sit leisurely on the couch, they might, at this very moment, be online with an older teen or adult who is sending them graphic pornography.

Denial suppresses concern; it ignores an instinct or sensitivity to signals that something is amiss. Because we want to be free from worry and fear, we close our minds (and our eyes) to the possibility of danger. We might feel concern about the way someone watches our child, but brush it off because we do not want to be skeptical of others. We feel uncomfortable that our children are in the basement unsupervised for a long period of time, but rather than check in on them, we tell ourselves it is silly to be distrustful.

Denial is an act of seeing something or sensing something is wrong but refusing to face it. It is sometimes an intangible feeling or observation we cannot yet articulate. It points to a concern, yet we ignore or reject it. Denial rationalizes away our valid apprehensions and lulls us into a false sense of comfort.

That perspective can lead to serious tragedy and a wealth of regret. Consider the story of a family who is invited over to the home of another family they know well. The adults are enjoying coffee while the kids are all playing downstairs in the family room. When it is time to leave, and the children come up, one of the boys mentions that his younger brother and another older child were alone in the bathroom together. The younger boy's mom has a moment of uneasiness. When she asks her young son about it, he acts sheepish, and the older child says he was helping her son wash his hands. The older boy's mother comments on how kind that was, and the other mom feels a bit embarrassed and has her son thank the older child.

It takes several other questionable moments and months later before another person walks in on the boys and sees the young child performing oral sex on the older child. The mother of the young boy later admits that she often felt uncomfortable with the older boy but did not want to be suspicious. That unwillingness to be "suspicious" cost her son months of suffering. We may not always know what we feel and why we feel it, but denial is never a good way to handle uncomfortable feelings and vague concerns.

Instead, we have to be willing to face that a threat to our children can be from someone they know and with whom they interact with routinely. We must be willing to believe that at some point our children might be approached, groomed, or targeted for ill intent. Accepting this reality should be the motivation you need to safeguard your children and your home.

Until children are old enough and have the skills to protect themselves, it is our responsibility to do so. Children who are given the responsibility of self-protection too early are ill-equipped for the task and often become fearful or hypervigilant. Children who have overprotective parents who shelter them grow up stifled, oblivious, and naive. Children who have loving, proactive parents who both protect, educate, and equip them grow up with safe parameters and resources to face the future confidently, wisely, and unafraid.

Our Confidence

As Jesus points out, worrying adds nothing; it does nothing (Matthew 6:27). Jesus goes on to say, "Therefore do not be anxious about tomorrow, for tomorrow will be anxious for itself. Sufficient for the day is its own trouble" (Matthew 6:34).

Remember: our confidence and trust must ultimately be in the Lord. We can be faithful to care for our children, protect them and equip them, and then we place them in our heavenly Father's hands. God is not only our refuge and help in times of trouble. God is also our children's refuge and help in times of trouble (Psalm 46:1). He is our shield and defender. He is our children's shield and defender too (Psalm 18:2). We do our job in equipping our children with the knowledge, discernment, and abilities they need to navigate hazards, then implore them to trust the Lord in time of need.

We want to shield our family against the dangers that exist, but we cannot shelter them from all danger. We can and should give them the knowledge and skills to know how to respond when problematic situations arise, preparing them to meet trials. Teaching them good from evil will put up a proper defense, protecting them against the arrows that are pointed their way.

As our children navigate an increasingly godless culture, it is even more important that our children are prepared to know how to think, respond, and live in the midst of it. If we do not equip them, they will fall prey to the snares set before them.

The apostle John reminds us of our hope: "Little children, you are from God and have overcome them, for he who is in you is greater than he who is in the world" (1 John 4:4). Do not be dismayed. Danger does exist, but so does light. As Christians, we are people who have a sure hope. Greater is he who is within us, than any evil that exists around us. And God is able to take what others mean for evil and uses it for good (Genesis 50:20).

It is our responsibility to be salt, to preserve what is good, pure, right, and holy–and to be light in the dark places.

As parents we can tend to approach the real dangers our world offers with either excessive fear and worry or with denial that danger exists. But as Christians, we always have another way available to us. Instead of anxiety, we go to God with all of our fears and ask for wisdom in how to navigate the dangers that surround us. Instead of denial, we face danger squarely, knowing we are not on our own, that God is with us and that he who is with us is stronger than he who is in the world (1 John 4:4). Our confidence is not in what we can do, but in our God who arms us for every good work. With that confidence we can equip our children to also put their faith in God as they learn to navigate the world we live in.

CHAPTER 3

Raising Equipped Kids, Not Fearful Kids

"Peace I leave with you; my peace I give to you. Not as the world gives
do I give to you. Let not your hearts be troubled, neither let them be
afraid." John 14:27

While it is important to acknowledge that our children face genuine
danger and that parents are called to protect them from harm, let's
also remember that we are called to raise equipped kids, not fearful
kids. We can educate our children about the dangers that exist without teaching them to respond with or live in fear. As I think about my
experiences as a parent and counselor, I would argue that the more
children are trained and given the tools to know how to respond to
uncertain or dangerous situations, the more confident, competent,
and at peace they will be.

Kids Who Fear

When our son turned five years old, we enrolled him in preschool. We
dropped him off every day and picked him up after work. One day
when we picked him up, his teacher mentioned that he had seemed
fearful and on high alert all afternoon. He would not play with any
of the children and stayed to himself in a corner. I asked if anything
had happened—was a child unkind to him, or did someone mistreat

him? The teacher could not point to anything that would have created his anxiety.

In the days to follow, this happened more often. He would ask us to pick him up sooner, or cling to us more in the morning and hesitate to enter the classroom. We talked with him often, asking if anyone had mistreated him, trying to draw him out. We noticed that even at church, he became hesitant to enter his Sunday school class and did not want us to leave him.

His behavior concerned us, and I began to worry we were missing something important. We struggled to know how to respond.

As we explored what might be going on, we discovered that every afternoon in preschool, two classes would combine as teachers were heading home. Our son's class was combined with children who were a year older. For whatever reason, that made him uncomfortable, even anxious. The same thing occasionally happened at church as well. We did everything we could to be watchful and ask good questions, while giving him the words to know how to speak if anything negative was occurring.

Over time, it appeared the source of stress for our son was discomfort with being with older children, though we had no reason to believe anyone was mistreating him. We did everything we could to ensure we were not putting him in a dangerous situation, and we worked to assure him he was safe, comforting him, and staying with him when necessary. Once we knew he was in a safe environment, we aimed to help him work through his anxiety by giving him skills to instill confidence.

I have to admit, I worried. I feared I might be missing something and that he might be harmed in some way. However, he gradually worked through this struggle, and I am happy to report nothing bad ever occurred.

However, as our son developed, he tended to have new fears and insecurities. He worried often about bad things happening to him. He was prone to be uncomfortable with new people and in new settings. He would occasionally talk about the idea of robbers and bad people kidnapping him. He had not experienced these things, but he was becoming aware of them. As he shared, we learned more about how his heart was prone to fear and how we needed to parent him. It became clear that he innately developed worries that needed to be addressed. We were given a window into what went on in his heart and the ways he felt vulnerable.

As parents, we must be aware that what we bring to the mix will either help or hurt our kids. How we approached our son would either instill more fear or help diminish it. We could have spoken in ways that dismissed his fears and made him feel disregarded, or we could use his fear to heighten our warnings against such dangers. Neither of these responses were a helpful or wise option. What he needed was for us to listen to his fears, protect him from true danger, and equip him to have the words, skills, and confidence to act, should he ever find himself in real trouble. He also needed opportunities to develop confidence within environments that we deemed safe.

If I allowed my concerns to take over and expressed my fear for him to him, I might have inadvertently affirmed his need to be afraid. Often a parent's reaction will heighten (or alleviate) a child's emotions. A child can learn to worry by watching how a parent handles fear and anxiety. But a child can also learn to relax by watching his parents' response to his or her concerns.

If you have a child that struggles with anxiety, you may be tempted to comfort your child by reassuring them, "Don't worry, that will never happen," or "You're fine; no one is going to hurt you or kidnap you." Though we can say these things with relative confidence, the reality is, the things our children fear *do* happen. Kids do get kidnapped, people do break into homes, and older kids do mistreat younger kids.

Kids are more informed and in tune with the world and local events than ever. They are often very aware, at too early of an age, of every danger out there. They hear it from the news, social media, a home device connected to the internet, or smartphones. And, if you have somehow buffered them from all of that, they will hear it from their peers, who are not protected and have constant access.

Do not provide false assurances to your children. Bad things do happen. Telling kids otherwise will either feel dismissive to them or they will determine you are irrelevant or inadequate to help them. In this world, there will be trouble. They will be exposed to it or alerted to it, and we must help them navigate it.

We do so in two ways.

First, we are always honest with them in developmentally appropriate ways. Children need to know their parents will be open, honest, and approachable when they're looking for truth. Our children need us to point them to Christ to make sense out of life. This starts by instilling a biblical worldview as they develop. This does not start in middle or high school with an apologetics course—it starts at two and three years of age, when we began teaching them about good and bad, how God made the world, and his design for families, relationships, and gender. It means we model talking about everything, and encourage questions. This practice continues throughout the course of our parenting as we disciple them in all of God's ways.

Our kids must be able to trust that they can come to us to help make sense out of their experiences. We do this by pointing them to the source of truth, to the One who makes sense out of life and their experiences. We share that when we ourselves are afraid and uncertain, we turn to the Lord as our refuge. We model a trust in the Lord. He is our source of wisdom and hope. We ultimately trust in his guidance and protection, and we talk about ways we see him at work in our own lives.

Second, we are tasked with equipping our children to face the realities of life and all the things they might experience. It is not enough to say, "Yes, the world is not safe, and you must trust God." Though true, it is incomplete. We must educate and prepare them to go out and engage with the world around them. We work to train and equip children with the tools to navigate life and all it will throw at them.

Deuteronomy 6 encourages us to teach what is good and right to our children as we go about life. We are to teach them diligently—talking with them when we sit and when we walk and when we lie down and when we rise up (Deuteronomy 6:7). We cannot always keep our children from exposure to evil or temptation, but we can equip them to respond to situations with wisdom and discernment.

Knowing Children and Where They Are Vulnerable

As our children develop, we must learn to pay attention to where they may have weaknesses or be prone to struggle. It is vital that we recognize ways these struggles may make them vulnerable, either to temptation or to being exploited. Young people can be vulnerable in many ways: age, stature, cognitive or emotional limitations, personal temptations, weaknesses, and disabilities, to name a few.

For example, children who are shy and nonassertive may struggle to stand up or speak out against bullying behaviors. They can be more readily targeted by other children who wish to take advantage of their timidity and bully them. Parents who understand this will work to help their child grow in assertiveness, be alert to the signs of a peer who bullies or tries to control them, and help them know who to go to or what to say in such situations. Parents can role-play, discuss, and provide options for how he or she can respond (see chapter 6 for more on the importance of role-play).

A boy's desire to be liked and accepted could make him susceptible to peer pressure or risky behaviors. He might be willing to be urged into disruptive behavior at school, may be encouraged to pick on another student to find acceptance in a group, or participate in risky behaviors like vaping, drugs, stunts, or criminal mischief to fit in with the football team. Helping your son see how fear of rejection could lead him to make unwise decisions and to sacrifice personal convictions is vital to preparing him to face such temptations.

A child with a cognitive disability may be led astray by an older student wishing to manipulate them. A teen girl who feels unloved or lonely may be susceptible to online exploitation. A child taught to trust and obey authority without question may be confused when sexually abused by a babysitter or grandparent. A young man with a physical disability is at the mercy of those who care for him. A toddler left in the care of a nanny or daycare is vulnerable in every way and will be completely dependent on others to care for them.

Caring parents can help to protect their kids by understanding their children's strengths and weaknesses, where they are prone to temptation, and what makes them vulnerable. In doing so, a parent can begin to personally speak into those places and guide their children individually. The more we understand our kids, the better we are at equipping them with the knowledge and tools they will need.

The Importance of Parental Discernment

When I was three years old, my sister had open-heart surgery in Philadelphia. My parents spent long hours in the hospital waiting with me, a then highly energetic three-year-old who was wearing them out. (I did circles around them and was known for leaping off furniture). Between concern for their baby who was in the middle of a serious surgery, and constant attention to their rambunctious child, they were exhausted.

My parents sat down in a waiting room and a lovely middle-aged woman struck up a conversation with my parents. Noticing they were tired and I was a handful, she offered to give them a break and take me for a walk. My mother felt something that did not sit right with her and was immediately on heightened alert. It is a red flag for a complete stranger to want to take a child out of their parents' sight. She politely declined. The woman asked again, assuring them it would be no trouble to help them out. My mom refused. Eventually the conversation ended and the woman left. Later that day, it was reported that a woman had taken off from the hospital with a toddler. The description matched that of the woman my parents had been talking to earlier.

Looking back, my mother was convinced that it would have been me kidnapped from the hospital that day. I personally am thankful she did not dismiss her concern as unfounded simply because she could not fully articulate the reason why. Rather than live with deep regret, we live with a story that illustrates the importance of paying attention.

We hate the idea of making false judgments about another person or their intentions, so we might easily dismiss a "weird feeling" as being paranoid. We may also do that in situations that make us nervous or uncomfortable.

Consider the person who approaches me while walking to my car and I become nervous. Or if I'm alone in a hallway at night with a stranger and I get worried. Or if someone gives me an unsolicited compliment, and I am wary. Am I paranoid? Overly suspicious? Cynical? Perhaps. How do you evaluate? I do not think our initial reactions are always trustworthy, but I do know that too often we are taught to overlook them, and too often we also teach our children to ignore such feelings.

A word I have found helpful when thinking about intuition is discernment. Discernment is an ability to judge or perceive something accurately. It is observing what is happening in the moment, though not always immediately clear, and trying to identify what you are seeing. Discernment picks up on many cues, details, and facts about a situation. It is a perception that something wrong or unsafe is happening, even though we cannot immediately articulate it in the moment. This is a skill we can teach our own children.

It is wise to stop, notice, and evaluate if a situation suddenly seems uncomfortable or "off" in some way. When given time to step back or process, we find we can often express what we were noticing.

Consider the many times we do this as parents. Perhaps you walk into room and immediately feel something is amiss. Your son is there and you ask what's going on. He says nothing, but seems a bit jumpy. You just sense something is "off." If you were in a hurry or preoccupied, you might just turn around and leave the room. If you slowed the moment down, however, you might suddenly begin to pick up on more details. The remote control was in your son's hand—was that it? Was he just watching TV when he should have been doing homework? You keep considering: he seemed jumpy and had a startled look on his face, he had a blanket covering his arms and you could not see what he was holding. The more you think about it, the more you realize he definitely looks tense and may be holding something in his hand.

You turn around and walk back in the room and ask to see what is in his hands. He pulls his hands out from the blanket, holding your cell phone. You take it out of his hands and open the history to find out he was watching pornography.

As you relay the story to your spouse, you are tempted to chalk it up to "mother's intuition" or a father's "Spidey sense." The reality, however, is that it was perception. You were recognizing multiple facts all at one time and you needed time to process what you were observing. Because you did not dismiss your sense of discomfort, you were able to stop and consider what you were noticing.

One of our kids always has a great "caught look" when he is doing something wrong. The average person might not notice it. It is there for a split second, then gone, but when I see it, I know what it means. He thinks I am a human lie detector. Little does he know that he is actually the one who gives it away; I am simply paying attention to him.

Parents and spouses often pick up on things that others may miss. It comes with years of living with a person and observing them. It comes from watching how they respond when they are angry, sad, excited, guilty, embarrassed, etc. It is seeing when they are genuinely surprised and when they are faking it. It is looking for signs they are hiding something or being transparent. The better we know our children, the better we perceive when they are struggling and press into their lives.

Discernment is a biblical word we can all resonate with. As mentioned earlier in this book, Hebrews 5:14 demonstrates that the mature have developed discernment through "constant practice to distinguish good from evil." Philippians encourages us to abound in love, with knowledge and discernment so that we might know what is excellent and pure (Philippians 1:9–10).

It allows us to discover truth, follow God's leading, and grow in good decision-making (Romans 12:2). It also helps us discern good from evil and malicious intent or motive from that which is virtuous

(Hebrews 4:12). There are those who are given the gift of discernment, but I am not referring to this practice in a way that presumes one must have a special gift of discernment. Rather, I am using the word the way Scripture calls us all to discern good from evil, right from wrong (Hosea 14:9). It is a willingness to observe, and sensitivity to what is occurring, even when we cannot put words to it. This produces insight and clarity; is modeled when both situations and people's behavior are observed and accurately evaluated.

In 1 Kings 3, the Lord asks the young, newly crowned King Solomon to make any request of the Lord that he wishes. Solomon's request is this: "Give your servant a discerning heart to govern your people and to distinguish between right and wrong" (1 King 3:9 NIV). The Lord is pleased with Solomon's request and responds, "I will do what you have asked. I will give you a wise and discerning heart" (1 Kings 3:12 NIV). Solomon knew that on his own he did not have the depth of understanding that would lead to discernment and wisdom. This can and must be learned and practiced through constantly distinguishing good from evil. It is also something we must be willing to model and teach our children.

Parents Must Seek to Grow in Wisdom

The practice of discerning right from wrong leads to a heart that is wise. The more we grow in understanding and knowledge, the wiser we will become. Proverbs 1:5 encourages us, "Let the wise hear and increase in learning, and the one who understands obtain guidance." We cannot separate growth in wisdom from growth in knowledge and understanding, and we cannot separate knowledge and understanding from the practice of discerning (distinguishing) right from wrong.

The wise person discerns good from evil and is eager to grow in knowledge and understanding.

We live in a world where evil, wickedness, immoral behavior, peer pressure, temptations, and trials are all knocking at the door. There will be forces at work to influence our kids toward godlessness. There will be those who seek to use and misuse your children—both adults and their peers. We know there are forces at work to lead our children astray—to deceive those who are naive, weak, innocent, or ill-prepared. How will we prepare them? The answer is by imparting knowledge and understanding that they may grow wise and discerning. We are called to ". . . test everything; hold fast what is good" (1 Thessalonians 5:21).

Will you remain silent and hope they aren't touched by it? If so, you are gravely naive. What your silence will do is demonstrate to your children that you were either inadequate or incompetent to help them. Will you circle the wagons, shrink their world, and keep them sheltered? If so, in the end, your desire to protect them will instead cripple them. They will lack the skill and discernment to respond to the temptations and dangers.

Will you put the proverbial "fear of God" in them, frightening them with the harsh realities of the perils that exist and encouraging a constant state of high alert? If so, you are causing the similar harm that you are hoping to protect them from. Young people who grow up with a persistent sense of anxiety are not prepared but hindered. Their fear renders them ill-equipped to discern between normal trials, minor concerns, and genuine danger. Instead, they live in a perpetual state of fear and alarm. Is that what you want for your children?

Living in a broken, fallen world means children will be exposed to evil, danger, and immorality. You cannot prevent all evil, but you can be equipped to guard against it and be ready to respond to it. We do not need to be controlled by a spirit of fear, but rather God has given us a spirit of power and love and self-control (2 Timothy 1:7).

The answer is discernment to know what is right and wrong, good and evil, and wisdom to respond. As Christians, we are to look for wisdom from our heavenly Father in the day-to-day and in the midst of trials. God gives wisdom generously when we ask. James reminds us that, "If any of you lacks wisdom, let him ask God, who gives generously to all without reproach, and it will be given him" (James 1:5).

A God-oriented discernment helps us in every area of life; the practical, the intellectual, and in the midst of suffering and blessing.

It orients us in how to navigate and respond in diverse situations. When we seek wisdom, God promises it will be found. In the chapters that follow, we will discuss how God-given wisdom and discernment can be applied to equipping your children with the safety skills they need in our world. Remember though, as you equip, to keep asking God for the wisdom you need and teach your children to do the same. Teach them and believe with all your heart that God will be their real safeguard.

Part Two

EQUIPPING CHILDREN
WITH SAFETY SKILLS

CHAPTER 4

Helping Parents to Recognize and Protect Children from Sexual Abuse

"A troublemaker and a villain, who goes about with a corrupt mouth, who winks maliciously with his eye, signals with his feet and motions with his fingers, who plots evil with deceit in his heart . . . "
Proverbs 6:12–14 (NIV)

Many parents worst fear is the abuse of their children at the hands of a sex offender. No parent wants to think about his or her child becoming a victim of abuse. But, although many parents fear it, few understand where the real danger lies and how to equip their children to handle this danger. We imagine a sexual predator is a creepy stranger who may lurk in dark hallways. However, reality says it is more likely to be someone we know, even someone we trust.

The pervasiveness of child sexual abuse can be difficult to verify since many instances are not reported. However, it is agreed upon by many that it is far greater than we might expect. Statistics may vary, but they remain fairly consistent when reporting the facts. One in four girls and one in thirteen boys are victims of child sexual abuse. The median age range of reported sexual abuse varies from age nine to as young as age two. Nearly 70% of reported abuse happens before the age of seventeen. In more than 90% of reported cases of child sex abuse, the children were victimized by someone they knew well.[8]

One study by David Finkelhor, the Director of the Crimes against Children Research Center, states these statistics:

- Just more than half of youth (530 per 1000) experienced a physical assault. The highest rate of physical assault victimization occurred between ages six and twelve.
- One in twelve (82 per 1000) youth experienced sexual victimization, including sexual assault (32 per 1000), and attempted or completed rape (22 per 1000).
- Child maltreatment was experienced by a little less than 1/7 of youth (138 per 1000). The study divided maltreatment into five categories (physical abuse, sexual abuse, emotional abuse, neglect, and family abduction) of which emotional abuse (name calling or denigration by an adult) was most frequent in occurrence.[9]

Parents tend to think of sexual offenders as some unknown individual "out there" prowling behind the schools and dark corners of society. It feels easier to deflect concern if the threat seems far from our children and easily recognized. If we believe a stranger, a hideous looking being, an obvious outrageous act, or an easily recognized "bad guy" is the primary threat, we may be lured into a false sense of safety when you don't see anyone like that in their lives.

But the sad reality is that evil intentions often hide in plain sight. Evil can and does masquerade as good, impersonates the upright; even the moral and virtuous. All the while, a person bent on sexual predation is often a master at concealing his or her intentions to gain access to a child for their own sexual gratification. Likely, we all have personally interacted with someone with the intent to harm a child, yet due to happenstance or careful watch, our child was spared harm.

With social media and the increase of children using technology, many avenues have opened up for those with malicious intent to gain access to our children. Parents can be so focused teaching kids about the danger of strangers, that we miss what is going on in the familiar settings of our own homes and communities.

Over and over, it is most often the people children know and interact with that will molest and harm, not the stranger. It is an aunt or uncle, a grandparent or older cousin, a babysitter you love and trust, or a youth volunteer you admire. It is crucial that we break down the mentality that the danger is "out there" somewhere. That belief prevents us from taking seriously the need to safeguard our children and our homes.

You as a parent will also be targeted. Those who wish to prey upon your children will seek you out and gain your trust. They will hold respectable jobs, look clean cut, and speak well. They will be nice, friendly, approachable, and charming. They will do everything to present as non-threatening, honest, and respectable as possible. They will build relationship and trust (with both you and your child) to gain access into your child's life. They work hard at gaining not only your child's trust, but also your trust and confidence. Child molesters know if a child were to tell, it would be hard for a parent to believe, if they had also gained the trust of the family.

Our initial response might be denial: "No way, not buying it. I would know." However, our confidence can blind us from accepting the nature of deception. This mentality blinds us from seeing the warning signs and cripples our children from knowing how to get help.

Anna Salter is an author and expert in the field of child sexual abuse, and she identifies our struggle to understand: "Character is the term we apply to the continuity we all want to see between public and private behavior. People act in accordance with their character—or so we think. 'He would never do such a thing' we say, shaking our heads. But 'character' ignores the real issue of deception. Even violent predators know enough to keep their behaviors in check publicly—most of them anyway."[10]

Scripture faces predatorial behavior head on: "For such men are slaves, not of our Lord Christ but of their own appetites; and by their smooth and flattering speech they deceive the hearts of the unsuspecting" (Romans 16:18 NASB).

Scripture gives us insight into what those who work in the field of child abuse are observing. Deceptive people with evil intent present certain ways. People will act one way, while plotting harm. They will deceive by speaking peace, while evil is in their hearts, they will try to win favor and charm you, but it is deceptive.

We can become wise and discerning to these things if we are willing to look at the uncomfortable realities. People deceive for different reasons: scammers deceive your family to gain money, a shady car salesman deceives to get a commission, an employee deceives to stay home from work, your daughter deceives you to go partying with friends, a son deceives to hide his poor grades. Deception can be found in all of us for varying reasons. But the intent of a sexual offender is far more grievous, and the consequences for a child are far greater.

We do not always know the reason someone deceives us, but we can become more discerning to the signs of deceit. We can pay closer attention to people's words and actions. We can begin observing patterns and behaviors that do not match up. We can notice when we feel uncomfortable or uncertain and stop to ask ourselves why.

An adult who sexually abuses a child does not wake up one day and decide to abuse a child. It is not an impulsive act, but evil desires that have been fostered and developed until one conspires to act. There are often years of corrupted desire that have gone unchecked and unaddressed. We cannot know what goes on in the heart, but we can know the signs when protecting our children from abuse.

We can equip and protect ourselves and our families by understanding both the nature of corrupted desires and the signs of deceptive behavior.

The Nature of Corrupted Desire and Deception

Temptation and desire exist within each of us. We cannot see inside a person's heart to know what temptations threaten to entice them, but we know that giving in to and fostering temptation gives birth to all types of destructive appetites and behaviors. The Bible explains it like this: "But each person is tempted when he is lured and enticed by his own desire. Then desire when it has conceived gives birth to sin, and sin when it is fully grown brings forth death" (James 1:14–16).

Scripture helps us understand how someone—even someone we know and love—can be enticed and corrupted by desire, and unchecked desire gives birth to sin. Desires become corrupted long before we can see bad behavior. We think something will tip us off; however, the nature of deception is to hide what is developing before actions demonstrate it.

Take, for example, a young person who is exposed to pornography. They do not know what to do or think, but it has elicited feelings and reactions they are ill-equipped to manage. If they don't go to an adult for help and interpretation, they will be left to make sense out of it themselves. Often, they slide into a struggle with lust. At what point will this be exposed? Will a parent be made aware? Now imagine that same child goes weeks, months, even years without anyone knowing—what does that do to him or her in the meantime?

In many cases, a young person who has been enticed by pornography searches for ways to act out the sexual acts they are viewing. This may be with a willing peer. It may be with a sibling whom they have immediate access to and can easily persuade. It may be with an adult they meet online who is seeking them out. The danger is not "out there;" it can even reside within us. Understanding this will help us accept the possibility that someone close to you is capable of being corrupted.

We cannot know what goes on in another person's life and heart, but we can choose not to be naive to it. You can choose to seek to understand the nature of self-deception, grooming, abuse, and a heart bent on evil. Once we are willing to consider such things, we can begin to prepare and prevent such things. The reality of danger, mistreatment, and abuse can cripple us with fear or push us to be equipped to recognize and respond. I want to encourage you to choose the later. You can be wise and discerning. You can also be equipped.

Warning Signs of Grooming

Since your child is more likely to be abused by someone they know and trust, how do you spot it? You need to be alert and watch out for what is called *grooming behaviors*—strategies used to build trust and lure a child into an abusive situation. Some of the following are examples of grooming:

- Gradual use of affection
- Treating a child like a peer
- Crossing of physical boundaries
- Bribes or gifts
- Special favors or attention
- Manipulation
- Filling or creating a role in the child's life
- Flattery, inflating a child's self-esteem
- Isolation and control over a child
- Increased reasons for spending time with a child

At first, some of these behaviors appear to be genuine acts of kindness. Any respectable, well-intentioned adult may do a number of these things: make a child feel special, compliment, build trust, etc. As a counselor, I work to build trust with young people, gain favor with their family, and spend time alone with a child. However, there are many things you and I would not (or should not) do: inflate a child's self-esteem, isolate or control a child, cross physical boundaries, etc. Intent and motives matter, but when uncertain, pay close attention to behavior. The more you are aware of behavior, the more it gives you freedom to distinguish motive. When uncertain, wisdom calls us to take precautions and limit the ability for awkward and inappropriate behaviors to continue.

When someone does attempt to groom a child, it may not be obvious at first. However, when you pay closer attention to who is involved in your child's life and why, you notice more. You might notice it is the third time your niece asked to take your son to the park alone. You notice the uncle holding your child on his lap more often than before, and how he seems a bit overly affectionate. You begin noticing and feeling less comfortable because you have given yourself permission to notice.

I use the word "notice" because it gives us permission to pay attention, to consider something that feels "off" or unnerving to us, and it gives us permission to then evaluate (or discern) what we are noticing. This could apply to the family friend who regularly asks to spend time alone with your son or daughter, the youth pastor who singles out a teen and begins showering them with gifts and special outings, the uncle whose affection makes you uncomfortable.

Precautions to Decrease Vulnerability

By virtue of age, size, and development, all children are vulnerable. But children with disabilities are even more vulnerable to sexual predators. Some of these children lack the same level of comprehension, discernment, or even physical strength that their peers have. Every child with a disability has different needs, vulnerabilities, strengths, and weaknesses. That means every child and situation is unique and requires a parent to be thoughtful, both in understanding the child's need for help and how you will best equip them.

Whatever our children's situation, there are precautions we can take to decrease children's vulnerability and keep them safe. We start by considering who the safe people are to help in caring for vulnerable children. This may be extended family, a pediatrician, teachers, or a childcare provider. Creating a plan is a good place to start when thinking about how to keep children safe from sexual harm, bullying, manipulation, or abuse. Being proactive, not fearful, will help both us and our children feel confident about safety. It's important to be thoughtful about how practical and capable a specific child is to follow through with the safety plan.

For example, if a child has cognitive limitations, you want to consider what you would teach them if they were alone at home and needed help. Is there a list of numbers to call, and would they know how to decide who to call? If a stranger showed up saying you had given them permission to enter the house, would they know what to do or say? If there was a fire, would they know the steps to take—how to call for help, where to go, or how to get out safely? If not, perhaps they are not ready to be left alone. You want to know that your child has the ability and knowledge to navigate such situations.

As a parent, you will want to make sure your instructions are as clear and concrete as possible. When directions are simple, they will know what to do and can easily follow steps, but they also need to be able to adapt to numerous potential pitfalls. If they are not to let anyone in the house, do they understand that rule also applies to people they know? Are there any exceptions to the rule, and do they know what these exceptions are and when? What do they do if they are uncertain? I will talk further on the subject in later chapters.

Parents should also talk openly with family and caregivers about the way we educate our children about sex and sexuality and about privacy and touch (see chapter 5 for more on this). Let your child's caregivers know you proactively teach and talk about these matters. It will make them aware that you are watching and care about such things. It will also help them to know what the expectations are, and how they can be part of keeping your children safe. Ask your child's caregivers to respect your child's personal space and to respect the level of care your child requires.

It is essential that your child learns how to ask for help—and who to ask. Young children, children with disabilities, and even the average student need to know how to ask for assistance. For example, if a child has a physical disability that requires help going to the bathroom. Role-play with your child who can help them, who they can approach for help, what help should look like, what help should not look like, and what to do if they are uncomfortable. If a fourteen-year-old gets lost in public or needs a ride somewhere, talk to them about how to make a good decision when getting in the car with a peer or accepting a ride from an adult and who they should contact before getting in a car with someone. The list could go on of what you might hope they would do or what you expect them to do when asking for or receiving help.

Address your child's specific vulnerabilities. Determine what the privacy level should be and what their comfort level is when allowing others to help them. Adjust your family guidelines and expectations to your child's specific needs. Perhaps a family rule is that no one should join your children when getting dressed. Yet for a child with a disability, they may require help. It is important to explain to other children why their disabled sibling will have an exception to the rule, and brainstorm how their unique needs can be accommodated in a way that keeps them safe. Invite siblings into the conversation so they can be part of the plan (when appropriate), serve as a resource for help, or to know when to report when something is amiss.

Role-play with your child what is okay and what is not okay. For example, if your child needs help in the restroom, clarify that it is okay for an individual to aide in unzipping her pants, help wiping, or help dressing her after using the toilet. However, explain it is not okay for a helper to pull her pants down or touch her genitals. Kids do not usually think about things that they have not experienced and can be caught off guard. Speaking clearly about what is and is not okay is very important in helping a child prepare for the unexpected.

Give other examples as well. If your child needs help with bathing and personal hygiene, it may be okay for a caregiver to help them undress, get in a bathtub or shower, or help them get out and dry off when needed, but it is not okay to undress anywhere else. Invite a child to have their own suggestions. Ask them to brainstorm things they might need help with, what would be helpful and good, and what would be wrong. Doing so will help your child recognize and reduce vulnerability to harm or abuse. Work with your children so you are consistent in how you teach what is good and respond to what is bad.

Your situation, your family and children may have varying degrees of maturity, abilities, or vulnerabilities that require you to take the principles outlined here and learn how to contextualize them to your home and circumstances. It takes time, thought, conversation and practice, but it yields worthwhile benefits. When you are uncertain, pursue help; God will give you wisdom and equip you for every good work. As you do so, remind your children (and yourself) that we are called to be wise and discerning, but at the same time to trust that God is our ultimate safeguard. Pray with and for your children that the Lord will give them discerning hearts and protect them from all kinds of evil. Making these issues a matter of prayer will teach your children (and you!) who to turn to for the help we need to wisely navigate our world.

CHAPTER 5

Teaching Kids to Evaluate Behavior

"For no good tree bears bad fruit, nor again does a bad tree bear good fruit, for each tree is known by its own fruit. For figs are not gathered from thornbushes, nor are grapes picked from a bramble bush. The good person out of the good treasure of his heart produces good, and the evil person out of his evil treasure produces evil, for out of the abundance of the heart his mouth speaks." Luke 6:43–45

Not long ago, I was taking my two boys to the pediatrician for their yearly checkup. The doctor was going through his normal routine of safety questions: Do you wear a helmet when you ride your bike? Do you wear a seat belt in the car? Do you know about stranger danger? My boys turned to look at me. I interjected, "Actually we don't teach our kids stranger danger, because it is a myth." "What do you mean?" he asked.

I explained that I was a counselor and research showed children were more likely to be abused by people they know, not strangers. Instead, we teach our kids *how* to talk to strangers. Should they ever be lost or need help, they will need to be able to approach someone they don't know to get help. We do not want our kids to be afraid of strangers; we want them to be equipped around strangers. There may be situations where they need to approach a stranger and ask for help, and they need to know what is appropriate to share or not share.

The statistics do not lie—children are more likely to be abused by someone they know than they are to be abused by a stranger. As mentioned previously, over 90% of the time, when children are molested, it's by someone they know personally.[11] Yes, abductions do take place, and kidnappings happen. However, time and time again, it is an uncle, stepparent, grandparent, cousin, nephew, pastor, neighbor, or coach who is approaching our children with wrong intentions.

It is also difficult for young children to know who is a stranger. Is the waitress in the restaurant a stranger? The bank teller or the store clerk? What about the mailman or neighbor down the street? Eventually, kids learn that either no one is a stranger, or everyone is untrustworthy. Neither option is helpful.

Author Gavin de Becker says this about never talking to strangers: "The rule is intended to provide protection in the event the child is alone somewhere, but because a parent is present, then what difference does it make if a young child speaks with a stranger? The irony is that if your child is ever lost in public, the ability to talk to a stranger is actually the greatest asset a child could have." De Becker goes on to say, "Children who are raised to assume all strangers are dangerous do not develop their own inherent skills for evaluating behavior."[12]

He makes as excellent point. If we are with our children and we are keeping them safe, then what is the harm in talking to strangers? In fact, it is an important skill for children to learn how to talk to people they do not know and what is appropriate to share. Not to mention, we are always breaking the rule when we ask them to tell the waiter what they want from the menu or have them talk to the cashier when paying for a toy. Basic, polite interactions are life skills we should be teaching our children. The ability to order a meal, ask for assistance in a store, or know when personal information should not be given, will help young people become adept at navigating social interactions. We need to model how and what to say to strangers we meet. Giving kids the confidence to engage well with people and know what is appropriate to share builds competence. It does not make them less safe, but protected and better equipped to ask for help should they find themselves in trouble and without us.

Learning to Spot Danger

We tell our children "Strangers are not dangerous; dangerous people are dangerous." Dangerous people can be a stranger or dangerous people can be someone you know—even someone close to you. How do you know if someone is dangerous? You watch their actions and listen to their words; you evaluate their behavior.

Too often, if we were to ask a child how to tell if a stranger is dangerous, they'd begin by describing the person's appearance: unkempt appearance, a scowling, sinister look on the face, excessively tattooed, or big and wearing dark clothes. Maybe they drive an old, beat-up car. Perhaps a child would then move on to describe the actions of a dangerous person. Such a person would, of course, act suspicious— devious even. They'd be manipulative, obscene, or attempting to inflict injury, right?

Wrong. Many immoral individuals will present as clean-shaven, well-dressed, polite, charming individuals but have malicious intentions. They will present themselves as likable, harmless, and normal. They will appear approachable, non-threatening and well-mannered. Whether it is an adult trying to gain access into your child's life, or one of your child's peers trying to befriend your son or daughter, a dangerous person will likely not fit the "bad guy" stereotype. Kids need tools to evaluate a person's behavior so they can discern whether a person is displaying good character or bad character.

I once read a book about spotting lies. It describes an interesting research project where a variety of professionals and people across the life span were evaluated for their ability to detect a lie. They researched with lawyers, FBI and CIA agents, professors, doctors, college students, teachers, etc. The outcome was very interesting. It found that FBI agents were no better at detecting a lie than a college student was.[13] Surprising, isn't it? It demonstrated how difficult it can be to read people well or detect deception.

Reading about and studying this subject has helped me work on the skill of noticing—listening to what people say and don't say, what someone is doing or not doing, that helps show me what is really happening in a situation. Yet, I am repeatedly surprised by the things I miss. My kids think I am a human lie detector, but they have certainly pulled the wool over my eyes many times. I think I know an individual, but then they do something that shocks me. The reality is we are not as perceptive as we would like to think. Accepting this will serve us well. It will be a reminder that we cannot always know what goes on in the human heart. We can only grow in discernment and paying attention.

Many parents whose child was molested struggle to understand how they could have missed it. How could they not have known the family member they loved or the minister they admired fooled them? So much of this shock is rooted in a belief that we can trust people we know and believe what they present to us. "They were always so kind." "They seemed so sincere and trustworthy." We tend to believe that someone's public persona is the real persona, or if it isn't, we'd somehow be able to tell. Two passages in Scripture illustrate this:

> . . . who speak peace with their neighbors while evil is in their hearts. (Proverbs 28:3)

> For such men are slaves, not of our Lord Christ but of their own appetites; by their smooth and flattering speech they deceive the hearts of the unsuspecting. (Romans 16:18 NASB)

When you and I accept that we can be fooled and are fooled by others, we are less likely to ignore concerning behaviors. We will be less likely to live in denial and more willing to face painful possibilities.

Evaluating Behavior

Years ago, my family was at a restaurant in a local mall. My husband and I, and our two daughters, sat in a booth while our youngest son, then two, was sitting in a highchair at the end. One booth away from of us sat two women having lunch. We ordered food and sat, chatting, and eating. The two women next to us sat eating and interacting, with the waiter moving back and forth between our tables.

About twenty minutes into our lunch, one of the women got up and began walking past us toward the bathroom, when suddenly she circled back around, leaned her arm over the booth behind me, smiled and said, "Hi, how are you all? I was wondering how much the salad bar was?" She then looked at my two-year-old son, caressed his cheek and said, "He's so cute. What's his name?"

I was caught off guard and also struck by the oddity of her questions, but I could not put together why. I glanced at my husband, who was taking a bite out of a burger, and looked back at the woman and shrugged and said I wasn't sure how much the salad bar was, but she could ask the waiter. She responded by repeating the question, "Oh, ok, he is really cute, what is his name?" She was patting his head.

Again, I glanced at my husband, who was still munching on his burger. Feeling even more uncomfortable but not fully understanding why, I found myself hesitant to know how to respond and stumbled out with something like, "You are making me uncomfortable." The woman responded, "Oh, well enjoy your meal." And went back to her table and sat down.

Warning bells were going off in my head, and as I stared at my husband for a response, one of my daughters piped up (loudly enough for anyone to hear), "Well, that was awkward!"

My husband was unfazed by the interaction. A harmless woman was chatting with us during lunch, in a public space. No harm done. I still felt uncomfortable and even suspicious about all of it, yet I could not initially form reasons why, until I began processing it out loud with him on the way home.

Why did it bother me, and did it even matter? Our son was never really in any danger. We were in a public place and both parents were sitting right next to him. My husband would have been a force to be reckoned with had she tried to pick up or take our son. I am so glad the end of the story was so anticlimactic, yet there was still something amiss.

An individual approached us under false pretense, though seemingly harmless. It would be easy to overlook that she was a complete stranger touching my son if I could explain it naturally by innocent interest or someone lacking social graces. However, looking like she is headed to the restroom, circling back around, and finding a question to ask that she did not really need answered, informs us that her motives were not what they appeared to be. She masked what she really wanted: personal information about one of our children. Did it matter that she wanted to know his name? I will never know because we did not offer it, nor do I know if it would have mattered if we did.

What I do know is she was not forthright, and her behavior and words demonstrated so. There were reasons warning bells were going off, though I could not articulate it in the moment. I did not have to figure out her motive, however; just evaluate her behavior.

Was our son ever in danger? Probably not. Was this person acting with sincere interest? Certainly not. Given the facts, it was right to respond with clear suspicion. I may not have known her agenda, and thankfully I did not need to. I only needed to consider what was actually occurring and respond accordingly.

Consider how many times you and I feel uncomfortable with something that is happening, yet because we can't fully articulate why, we are quick to dismiss it as illegitimate. We tell ourselves that our concerns are unfounded. Our willingness to discount concerns because we cannot explain motive can lead to nothing more than an anticlimactic end to an interaction (as in my story), but it could possibly lead to tragic outcomes. It is far better to take steps to avoid a potentially harmful situation when you wonder what someone's intentions were, than to live with the regret of ignoring your concerns and finding out they intended harm.

We must be willing to notice things that seem amiss, while always being aware that we may not know what to do with what we notice. You do not want to be an alarmist, nor do you want to overreact. Perhaps the best approach is to start with a willingness to notice. This means being willing to step back and observe what is happening. We don't need to immediately assign value, good or bad; we are simply willing to pay attention and ask more questions.

We can see how a young child or even a teenager would not innately have such skills in discernment. It comes with training and practice. This is why as parents we must teach our kids tools to evaluate unusual behavior.

Note that the key is to evaluate behavior, not character. People who are intending to deceive will try to present themselves as sheep: innocent, harmless, friendly, and trustworthy. It is not immediately clear, but if we learn to watch, listen, and evaluate, their actions will betray their motives.

Jesus tells us to evaluate people not by how they represent themselves but by what they actually do. The good person, he says, will do good. The evil person will do evil (Luke 6:43–45). He calls what people actually do the "fruit" of their lives. The "fruit" or behavior in a person's life will reveal their true character. Young people need the skill of evaluating people's words and actions to determine trustworthiness, and even then it can be challenging.

When Children Can and Must Defy Someone in Authority

Teaching young people to evaluate right and wrong helps them begin to stand up to negative influences, whether it is from a peer or an adult. We spend much of our time teaching children obedience and compliance (as we should), but we also need to teach them when they can and must defy someone in authority—or in any position.

We began modeling this principle to our young children by telling them this:

"If someone tells you the right things to do, you should *always* listen. It doesn't matter if it is grandma, Uncle Dave, the babysitter, your coach, your younger sibling, or the family dog (for fun effect!). If it is the right thing to do, you should always do it, no matter who is telling you. What's the principle? Doing what is good and right is more important than who is telling you to do it."

Likewise, we go on to say, "If someone tells you the wrong thing to do, you should never do it, and we will support you—whether it is your teacher, coach, Sunday school teacher, sibling, friend, or grandfather. If it is wrong, you never have to listen, and we will support you." The principle here is if something is wrong, you never have to comply, no matter who it is. Kids learn that with disobedience comes consequences. Therefore, it is imperative that our kids know we will always support them if they defy authority for good reasons.

This is where encouraging conversation and role-playing becomes so important. It is not enough to simply say, "If someone tells you something wrong to do, you should never do it and we will support you." We must continue to say it, give examples, and let them ask questions.

Since we are (hopefully) surrounding our children only with those who are telling them the right thing to do, it can be confusing to a child to know or believe they have our permission to defy authority. That's why it is necessary to model for them what those situations could look like. Here are some examples:

Pick the name of a relative or someone they know well.

Parent: "If Kim, the babysitter, tells you the wrong thing to do, you never have to listen, and we will support you. Meaning, we will not be angry with you, nor will you get in trouble for refusing to obey."

Child: "Kim wouldn't tell us to do anything bad."

Parent: "I hope not, and she is a good babysitter. But if she did tell you to do something bad, you never have to listen, and we will support you. What might be some bad things Kim would ask you to do?"

Child: "I don't know. Lie?"

Parent: "Yes, maybe. What type of things might she (or anyone) have you lie about? Maybe she lets you stay up later than we asked or gives you dessert and tells you to lie to us. What else could she say or do?"

Child: "Maybe she tells us we can do something we know you would not let us do, or is not safe, like play in the garage near Daddy's tools?"

Parent: "Good! Yes, things like that. Now, what if she told you to hit your sibling?"

Child: "That would be bad!"

Parent: "Right! And you could refuse. Just like if she told you to take something you're not allowed to have. Now, what if she told you to go running down the middle of the street clucking like a chicken or smear peanut butter in your sibling's hair?"

Child laughing: "That's silly. She wouldn't do that!"

Parent: "Probably not, but if she did, you should never listen. What might be some other silly things she tells you to do?" Have kids brainstorm ideas.

Parent: "What if she asked you to take your clothes off in front of her? Or asked you to take a shower with her?"

Child: "Ewwww, she wouldn't do that; that's bad."

Parent: "Yes, it is bad, and I hope she never would. But if a grown-up like Kim, or Grandpa, or a cousin ever asked you to do any of these things, you should always say "no" and go tell us or another grown-up right away. We will always support you."

As an adult, you are putting forth the possible ways someone might encourage them to do wrong: from the improbable or the silly, to the serious and scary scenarios. Then, watch how your child responds to each of these scenarios. It will reveal their tendencies to react or not react, and it will reveal where they may be vulnerable. It will also help you know how to shepherd them through such situations.

You can turn it into a game called "What Would You Do?" Everyone takes turns creating scenarios, trying to brainstorm what the right thing to do would be. It is essential you use common, everyday situations and then move on to describe situations they might not be able to fathom, but could happen. Let the kids come up with their own as well. Kids often will draw from their own experience, so you can learn the things they are facing with peers and in their day-to-day life.

Follow up with asking questions or allowing them to try to stump you with "What would you do?" situations. One of my sons was notorious for trying to poke holes in my logic. He would say things like: "Well, what if we don't know if what they are asking us to do is good or bad?" I would respond with, "Great question. What might be some examples of that?" We brainstorm and think through the possibilities together. And when all else fails, tell them, "If you don't know if what a person is doing is right or wrong, go find another grown-up and ask them." That invites other adults to have eyes on the situation and step in when needed.

What is happening here? Kids are learning to evaluate right from wrong, no matter the person in the scenario. For some of us, this feels counterintuitive. If I talk to kids about hard things, won't I instill fear in them? Won't they be more afraid? No, it is quite the opposite. When parents do this well, kids do not learn to be afraid, because we are not modeling fear. With the guidance of safe, loving parents and adults, kids are educated and equipped for potential troublesome situations. They are becoming competent to face life's challenges.

More Ways to Help Kids Discern Problematic Behavior in Others

What might be some problematic behaviors to notice in a peer or an adult? Here are a few:

- When behavior is forced upon another individual
- When a child is too rough, either through rough play or forced affection
- When someone joins you when you are changing clothes

- When someone urges them to go to private or unseen places, like restrooms, sheds, tents, under playground equipment, behind parked cars, etc.
- Pressure or intimidation of any type
- When someone persists in aggressive physical contact, doesn't respond to social cues, or ignores the word "no"
- Bullying behaviors, like taking someone's food, money, or possessions, pushing them around or making fun of or mocking others
- Sexual talk or inappropriate behaviors
- Reckless behaviors, like abuse, drugs, vaping, smoking, etc.
- When others try to make you keep secrets from your parents or trusted adults

Some kids have a natural curiosity or struggle with social skills. They are not unsafe, but perhaps at times inappropriate. Helping your children be sensitive to individuals like this is the kind and right approach to take. It means giving them the ability to consider that another person may do something inappropriate while not trying to be inappropriate. The behavior is still problematic, and your son or daughter may still rebuff it, but not because they are unsafe. Kids who are taught to understand the difference between kids who struggle to understand social cues and norms from those who purposely ignore the feelings and boundaries of others will naturally start to perceive this. They will more easily notice when behavior is potentially unsafe and when it is improper socially. Consider Proverbs 20:11 that states, "Even a child makes himself known by his acts, by whether his conduct is pure and upright."

When a pushy child tries to take away a toy from your daughter, you can (and should) encourage her by prompting her with, "Honey, it is okay to say, 'Please don't take it—I am still playing with it.'" When she is too shy or afraid, or struggles with assertiveness, you can step in and say so for her. Modeling a wise way to respond to wrongdoing at any age is important.

See Something, Say Something

Teach your kids that if they see anything that makes them uncomfortable, you want to hear and help them process it. Sometimes children feel uncomfortable, awkward, or afraid and cannot always put it into words. Other times, kids know another individual is making bad choices, participating in risky, dangerous, or clearly immoral behavior. Let them know that regardless of whether they know if it is good or bad, it is okay to go to a trusted adult and ask for help.

If that adult does not listen and they still need help, tell them to keep going to adults until someone will listen and help them.

One of our children was in an afterschool program when they were younger. There was another child who was aggressive and often bullied other kids. One afternoon, while our son was playing, this child decided to pick on him. He was provoking him, trying to mess up something he was building, and calling him names. We taught our son when this happens, to go tell an adult, and if that adult does not listen, go find another adult, and keep doing so until someone listens.

This was just such an occasion, and he did just that. He told three different adults. Unfortunately, they did not stop the behavior. They briefly talked to the child, then went on to tend to other responsibilities. The boy did not leave our son alone, instead he continued to provoke him. Our son ended up defending himself, landing both himself and the one doing the bullying in the principal's office.

We taught him the right thing to do, and sadly, he felt unheard. He then took matters into his own hands, and given the circumstances, I can't say we blamed him. His response was, "I kept telling the grown-ups, and it didn't stop." Regardless of how you feel about your child defending themselves against bullying behaviors, you must have the conversation. Your child needs to be prepared to know what to do, who to go to for help, what to do if no one comes to his aid, and how you expect him or her to defend themselves should they need to.

Likewise, if they are concerned about the behavior of an uncle, parent, cousin, sibling, or other family member, always have them tell someone safe and keep telling until someone listens and intervenes.

Encourage Open Communication at Home

Parents must take the lead in modeling openness and freedom as they talk about such topics. It may be uncomfortable to you, but it does not need to be hard or complicated. Talk regularly with all family members in the home—children, teenagers, and adults—about appropriate and inappropriate behavior to ensure they understand and remember the information.

Consider these principles:

- Set clear family guidelines for personal privacy and behavior. Discuss the guidelines with all members of your family, why you have them, and model respecting these guidelines.
- As a child develops, restrictions may need to change (e.g., knock on the door before entering, asking for a hug, guidance on appropriate wrestling with one another, or joking).
- Discuss these guiding principles with any other adults who spends time with your children (e.g., if a child likes affection or does not want to kiss or hug, what language you use, and other expectations you have).
- Let children know that if they are not comfortable being around someone, then you will help them figure out why and what to do.
- Encourage discussion as a family and invite kids to ask questions or come to you later if they'd like to talk more about something that is bothering them.
- Learn about the resources in your community (who to talk to in school about drugs or bullying, what to report if you see something happening in your neighborhood, when to report suspected abuse, etc.). Know who to contact should you need to report something.
- Help kids know if they see something troubling, to say something. It may not be clear what is going on, but bringing it to someone's attention helps prevent concerning behavior to be overlooked.

- Make a list of resources for your family to use when parents are absent—names and phone numbers of emergency services and why and when they would call them. Place it somewhere easy to access for young people. This may be the fire company, poison control, the local police department, etc.
- Make sure everyone knows that they can talk with you about any inappropriate behavior that may already have occurred; that you love them, won't be angry with them, and will work to get them help.

Implementing these principles will equip your children to do what 1 Thessalonians 5:21 implores: "But test everything; hold fast what is good." By doing so you are giving them the tools to evaluate behavior and to discern problematic situations and people even when on their own. But you are also opening the door for them to come to you with any concerns or any behavior that seem off to them even if it is from an authority figure or another trusted person that they are familiar with. Beginning to have these conversations means you are well on your way to instilling discernment in your children. In the next chapter, we will expand on these suggestions to talk more about the value of practice and role-playing, and why it can be helpful to your children.

CHAPTER 6

Practice Makes Permanent— Using Role-Playing to Disciple Children

"And these words that I command you today shall be on your heart. You shall teach them diligently to your children, and shall talk of them when you sit in your house, and when you walk by the way, and when you lie down, and when you rise." Deuteronomy 6:6–7

How do we teach our children good from evil? How do we teach them to evaluate behavior—to know themselves, and to know what's right and what's wrong? God tells us what's right and what's wrong in his Word. God also commands us to teach our children diligently and consistently about him and his ways, so that it will permeate every area of our lives. Constant conversation and practice connect biblical principles to everyday lives. Role-playing with your children is a great tool for creating opportunities to have meaningful and fruitful conversations that disciple them in God's ways. This kind of discipleship will help children to recognize and turn from what they might do naturally or what the world tells them to do.

Role-playing is when you present a situation to your children and ask them what they would do and say as they take on different roles in the story. For example, your child may not know what to do when a peer pressures him to lie or cheat. Role-playing gives children an avenue in which to practice possible responses to difficult situations.

It allows children to think with you about situations they haven't encountered. This will also help you understand how your children think by providing a window into their fears, into areas of temptation they grapple with, and into situations in which they might be caught off guard or be vulnerable.

When our girls were four and five years old, they trusted everyone. We saw early on that they would be willing to walk off with anyone who invited them. So, we began role-playing with them about what to do if they were approached by someone who lost a puppy or offered them candy. We would explain that if anyone ever wanted them to go somewhere with them, the first thing they should say is, "I have to go ask my Mommy or Daddy first." Then we would role-play. I would say something like, "Hi little girl, I lost my puppy. Can you help me find him?" Or, "Hello, I have some candy in my car and I am giving it out to kids in the neighborhood. Would you like to come pick some?"

To my dismay, they would fall for the ploy over and over again. I would walk through what to say and then have them practice. Slowly, over many practice sessions, they would pick up on it. We would practice at home, at a local store, or at a park while they were playing. I'd walk up to one of my children and say something like, "Hey little girl (they knew this was the cue for role-playing), I have some kittens in my car I want to give away. Do you want to come see them?" My oldest would light up, then think for a moment and say, "Oh no . . . not unless I talk to my Mommy." I would smile, congratulate her, and give her a big hug. It was always lighthearted, fun, and instructive, never punitive if she gave a wrong answer.

It was also instructive to me as it taught me where my kids might be vulnerable or easily swayed. My next child, when asked if she would like to have some candy, would regularly cave to the temptation. We'd role-play over and over until one day her answer was: "Well, what *kind* of candy is it?" Though she knew the right response, it became clear that she could be enticed if the reward was worth it. This proved to be true again and again, but the role-plays did help us understand and better parent her in light of her temptations and weaknesses.

More Ways to Foster Open Communication

I have found that the more I am willing to talk about the many "what ifs" with children, the more they are willing to say, "I don't know. What do I do when that happens?" This kind of role-playing becomes an open door for discipleship. By asking your children questions that encourage them to think and make decisions, you help them to not be stuck in a situation where they don't know what to do. Inevitably our children will get stuck, but role-playing and intentional conversation will decrease these occurrences. You are giving them the skill of evaluating circumstances and people. While you teach them right from wrong, they learn to perceive, judge, and problem solve.

As your children mature, don't forget to encourage them. You won't always get it right and neither will your kids. It's important to tell children, "Do your best and we will be proud of you. And if you do get it wrong, we will talk about what happened." This assures children that they won't be punished for trying to apply what they've learned from you. Often refinement is what is needed, not punishment.

We cannot possibly come up with every scenario our children will encounter, but regular practice will help them develop discernment. If we teach them to stop and think about what is happening and then rehearse with them, they will learn the skill of evaluating situations. When we encourage them to regularly evaluate behavior, they will grow, develop, and demonstrate an ability to read people and situations.

I encourage you to incorporate these types of conversations into normal everyday life. I have found that our van is a good place to get my kids talking about these "what ifs?" The car is an undistracted place for kids to reveal their thoughts and experiences, and the ride gives you time to help process and interpret those experiences. But anywhere you can get your kids to talk with you about different situations is a good place: mealtime, bedtime, or walking through a store. Seeing a tense situation unfold in front of you is a great time to turn to your kids and make it a teachable moment. I'll often say, "Hey guys, what did you think about that? What did you think about how that person handled the situation? How would you respond?" As parents we need to be on the lookout for teachable moments and also take on the responsibility of proactively creating opportunities for conversation through activities.

Learning to Apply Biblical Principles

Since kids tend to think in black-and-white terms it can be challenging for them to wisely navigate the gray areas in life. Children may understand biblical principles, but struggle to apply them in the moment. Role-playing is an opportunity to take teachable principles—demonstrating love, kindness, mercy, forgiveness, assertiveness, safety—and transfer them into different situations. This type of conversation primes children to take one principle and apply it to a multitude of contexts they might not have considered. It helps expand their understanding of the principle as they see it applied to different contexts, and it prepares them for the many situations that may (or may not) happen. As you use this tool, you provide a spectrum of possibilities: from the silly, to the obvious, to the confusing, to the dangerous, to a scenario that seems impossible.

For example, it is possible your child could be an aggressor in one situation (bullying or sexting) and then be pressured or attacked in another (online grooming or sexual assault). Most children are not always the bully or always the one being bullied. So, develop a scenario where your child is tempted to be an aggressor (maybe with a younger sibling) so you can speak about love and respect for others. Then develop a scenario in which your child is the one being mistreated and walk through how to respond and get help.

You can start by making these conversations simple and natural. Perhaps you ask your child if they know anyone at school who is a bully. You ask them what behavior they notice that makes this peer a bully. Ask if they have ever been mistreated this way and ask what they would do if they were? Brainstorm ways they could respond to a bully and ask them which response feels easiest or most natural for them. Some children will have no problem being assertive and standing up to others and may need help doing so in ways that are respectful. Other children may struggle greatly with speaking up for themselves or others and will need to be given the words, encouragement, and confidence to speak up. Proposing various situations and having your child practice what they would say, will impress upon them the words and courage they need.

Here are some suggestions:

- What if your friend pressures you to share your test answers when no one is looking? How can you respond?
- What if you see a peer being mistreated on the playground? What should you do?
- A student is mocking you for the clothes you wear and provokes others to make fun of you as well. What are ways you can respond?

The list could go on with possible scenarios, as well as options of responding. Growing in wisdom means that you seek to understand what is happening, know where your child might wrestle with reacting, and begin to equip your son or daughter with a godly response. Some children will need you to suggest the words and language to communicate. Other children may need you to brainstorm with them options and/or solutions, so they can know what response might be helpful in each situation and what response could be unhelpful—or even make things worse.

Know Your Child and Encourage Self-Awareness

When we try to instill values in our children, we are also trying to help draw out their own hearts. When helping a child evaluate friendships, help them understand why they are drawn to certain groups of friends, what they value or admire in their peers, where they are tempted to find identity or acceptance, as well as to what lengths they will go to attain it.

The more you understand them—their strengths, weaknesses, temptations, fears, insecurities, dreams, and desires—the more it will help you identify their vulnerabilities.

Consider these all-too-common examples:

- The son feels lonely and different due to a learning disability, and you notice he spends much of his time online gaming. He escapes into video games and finds it easier to talk to kids in this online format, so he lets his guard down. He is vulnerable to trusting faceless individuals who pursue him and attempt to gain his trust, slowly gathering personal information from him.
- The daughter who struggles with her appearance. She looks at the world around her to figure out how she should feel about herself. She turns to social media to inform her on what is considered attractive, how she needs to dress, apply her makeup, and how thin she must be. She fluctuates between an eating disorder and self-hatred, and seeks constant affirmation online to feel good about herself. She is only nine years old.
- The young boy who is small for his age and grade. He is timid and nonassertive, which has opened him up to bulling behaviors. Older kids begin to tease him on the bus and take his lunch before he makes it to school. How will you help him navigate this?
- The teenage jock who desperately wants to make the wrestling team. The team is known for crude behavior and drug use. He is tempted to conform so he is accepted as one of them. He is mocked when he talks about having a curfew or going to church.

A parent who proactively disciples their child will be alert to these struggles and will (hopefully) actively enter into their child's experience to help them. We cannot always stop a struggle from unfolding, but we can be aware and proactive in guiding them through it. The more we understand them, the more we are able to help them make sense of their struggles.

Work to teach your children the skill of self-reflection. Once they start to talk, urge them to consider their motives for what they said or did, and gently challenge their responses to stimulate critical thinking and greater self-awareness. If we want to raise godly children, these skills are essential. The more they do this, the more discerning they will also be of others.

Be Your Child's Safe Person

For our children to discern safe people from unsafe people, you and I must model it. Your child will learn mature, healthy, good relationships first and foremost by seeing it lived out before them. How you conduct yourself both publicly and privately are the greatest models of moral character and behavior you can give your children. The more they see what is good and right and true and lovely (Philippians 4:8), the more they will be put off by those things which are not.

Children are being groomed by our culture and outside sources to accept evil as good and their parents as irrelevant. Work hard to prove your value and win a place in their hearts. The more you demonstrate you are a safe person to open up to, share with, and talk to, the more profound your influence will be—especially when they are struggling.

How we parent, provide guidance, implement discipline, demonstrate affection, speak to one another, and engage with those with whom we live and work, is how our children will learn and evaluate such things. Every time you treat them with respect and dignity, you demonstrate what a safe person is. Every time they see you help a stranger, be patient with the elderly, or return an insult with kindness, they learn how to respond to those situations in their lives. Every time they observe you stand up for someone being mistreated, rebuff a pushy salesperson, or ignore an aggressive driver giving you a not-so-friendly gesture, they learn how to handle offensive behavior.

When kids sense a parent is uncomfortable or awkward about something, they learn to avoid bringing it up. Kids need to see their parent talking about the hardest topics—sex, sexuality, abuse, war, death, etc.—with calm repose. We may not always feel so relaxed, and may even feel anxiety over a subject, but what kids need to observe is a parent who can put that aside for their children's sake and demonstrate comfort with any topic their children may need to bring to them. We show we are safe by being able to handle any hard thing our children might bring to us.

Being their safe person does not mean we always know what to say, nor do we have all the answers. It is fine to say, "That's a hard question, let me think about it and get back to you." You can tell them you'll research a question they have, as long as you return to them with a willingness to continue the dialogue. All of this signals to our children that we are approachable, willing, and engaged with their lives and struggles.

Other Safe People: Talk about Who They Can Go To

Identify several people in your child's life you would feel comfortable with them going to if they needed help, and would struggle coming to you, or if you were not available. This may be another family member, a person at school, or a youth leader. Talk through what would make them safe or unsafe and what to do if for any reason that person made you uncomfortable. If one person makes them uncomfortable, they can approach the next adult for help.

You always want to be your child's primary safe person, but sometimes you may not be present, readily available, or perhaps they may be afraid to come to you. If that happens, you want to know that you both have identified people you would be comfortable with them going to for help, and that they are equally comfortable with the same individuals. It is not helpful having you pick their safe people if they are unwilling to go to them when in need. Having loving, safe, reliable adults for a child or adolescent is crucial, as well as a great resource for mentoring/ modeling relationships.

Practice Makes Permanent

Perhaps you are already tired of hearing me say you must role-play and practice. But it just makes sense. Good teachers see this all the time. The kids who have practiced their spelling words or multiplication tables are more prepared to react when called on. The answer comes readily and without much thought because they have internalized the information. When given a word problem in math, a child who has learned the basic skills and been practicing will be able to stop, think, and figure it out, as opposed to a child who has never had to consider a word problem and has no idea where to begin.

You've heard the old adage, "practice makes perfect." Years ago, one of my sons came home from school and said, "Mom, do you know practice really makes permanent?" He then proceeded to explain to me what his teacher had taught him: if you learn to do something the wrong way (and repeatedly do it the wrong way) you will learn permanent bad habits, which will likely result in bad outcomes. If you learn the right thing, and practice it, you will have permanent good habits.

I mulled over his statement for a while and realized this rang true in many areas of life. I decided to turn it into a teachable moment to talk to my kids about ways we do this in our spiritual lives, thought lives, and social relationships.

As we teach our children various behaviors and habits, our focus is often only about external behavior. Our instruction centers on what to do and when to do it, without any real connection to why. Ultimately, everything our children do should stem from what is good and right. We teach a love for God and others. (I love my sister, so I allow her to choose the movie, or I love God, so I show gratitude for the belongings I own.) We want to teach our children to do good things—for godly reasons. This informs the motives behind our behavior as well as the attitude.

What Is Becoming Permanent?

Good habits, behaviors, and even spiritual disciplines can become permanent rituals done for duty's sake only, rather than resulting from a relational choice to love. It is important to realize that even good things like respect for others can become a practiced obligation (i.e., "the right thing to do") with permanent, loveless effects.

Consider Christian practices: prayer, regular church attendance, and Bible reading. If we do these things only because we are "supposed to," they will become rote, obligatory, and eventually meaningless tasks because they are disconnected from personal, loving relationships with God or others.

I have worked with countless children who know the right response to a difficult situation, but when pressed, they have little or no expectation that it will actually accomplish anything. For them it is merely a forced habit, void of relationship, with no expectation that God is really there at the other end. If we aren't careful, these children will grow up believing that because prayer does not always produce a change in circumstances, it must not work at all. And if we do not also teach them how to respond to mistreatment (when to walk away, when to stand up for what is right), they come to believe they must passively accept mistreatment from others.

Instead, we need to teach safety skills out of a relational context, with God as our Father, modeling how to ask for his help during hard moments and learning from him how to respond to evil. Children will see that God is with us and will strengthen us. This builds up our confidence in God and spills over into other relationships and situations.

What Should We Be Practicing?

We must be committed to teaching our children (and reminding ourselves) that everything we do—whether practicing loving responses to others, standing up for those who are being mistreated, or learning personal safety skills—all must be done out of a conscious decision to live our lives based on God and his ways. God cares about what is right and good and just.

It is from this personal conviction that we choose to steward our life well before the Lord. In teaching this truth—that all life is lived before God—we are impressing on our children a different way of thinking, a different rationale for living that will serve them well when they struggle to respond to new situations.

My hope is this: that God would help us model and practice with our children the delight of living in relationship with him and having a healthy, loving view of relationships that equip them for life. Doing so builds competent children who know how to relate to people, whether it is to extend kindness and help, or to guard against being mistreated. What an excellent practice to become permanent in our homes!

CHAPTER 7

Key Topics to Discuss with Children

"Whoever gives heed to instruction prospers,
and blessed is the one who trusts in the LORD.
The wise in heart are called discerning,
and gracious words promote instruction."
Proverbs 16:20–21 (NIV)

Too often parents shy away from difficult conversations with their kids. We avoid discussions about sex, sexting, sexual abuse, date rape, drinking, drugs, bullying, online pedophiles, and much more. We sidestep the uncomfortable or frightening topics we do not want to face. We put off challenging conversations, often out of our own inadequacies or discomfort.

Perhaps you feel ill-equipped—you know your children will face these issues, but you don't know how to broach the subject with your child. You know it needs to be addressed, but hoping your child is not yet facing these risks, you put off the conversations for as long as possible.

When it comes to talking about challenging or uncomfortable topics, remember that God calls you to instruct your children—to teach them to trust God and be discerning. Your words don't have to create anxiety in your child. They can be gracious and full of grace as you raise difficult topics in a way that demonstrates you have insight and instruction to offer your children. It is far better to proactively shape how they view any given subject than to try to go back and debunk inaccurate views.

You may worry that if you talk to your children about sex, risks in dating relationships, or online pedophiles, that you'll incite fear in them. But that doesn't have to be true. How your children respond depends on *how* you talk to them. Kids are inundated all day long with images on their devices, television, commercials, schools, billboards, and the like. They will be peddled images of love, romance, sexuality, friendships, brokenness, good, bad, identity, and normalcy. They will be making sense out of these things. The question is, will they do it with or without your guidance?

Children who are taught God's ways and given discernment about good and evil do not need to fear uncomfortable topics. Instead, they can be equipped, at ease, and knowledgeable, engaging rightly with the messages they will see and hear around them.

Talk with Your Kids about Abuse

As parents, you want to do what you can to make sure your children know what concerning behaviors look like. When children are being abused, there are signs a parent can learn, but children can also be victimized in ways that are not, at first glance, tangible. Children can be shown pornography, be recorded unawares, or be spoken to or asked to dress in sexualized ways. All of these things may not involve touching but clearly are abusive to a child.

The more you have talked about respect for each other's bodies, privacy, developmentally appropriate conversations about sex and sexuality, and who may help a child dress or bathe, the more likely your child will be to shield themselves or speak up when mistreated.

Talk with Your Kids about Sex

The Scriptures tell us that all life comes from God. Psalm 139 says, "For you created my inmost being; you knit me together in my mother's womb. I praise you because I am fearfully and wonderfully made; your works are wonderful. I know that full well." (vv. 13–14 NIV). This truth might seem self-evident to Christian parents, but is has important implications. God knit each person together and created them in his image. There is no shame in how they are designed. This is significant as we talk to kids about gender, their bodies, and sexuality.

Respect and Privacy

Frequently we approach the subject of sexuality with trepidation and awkwardness. Our own discomfort, experiences, and beliefs about these issues inform how we do (or don't) educate our children. You may need to evaluate how your own struggle with this topic needs to be transformed so it does not get in the way of teaching your kids a healthy, biblical understanding of sexuality.

For example, words like "wee-wee" and "girl parts" may seem more comfortable and harmless, but it also can presume shame or inadvertently send a message that private body parts are too embarrassing to mention by name. Using words like penis, vagina, breasts, behind, or rear end are accurate names for our body parts and there is no need for shame or embarrassment when we use them.

We seem to have an unhelpful aversion to talking about parts of the body that seem taboo, and that message is caught by our children. We need to be aware of our own discomfort and be willing to change. We can and should model speaking in respectful ways when it comes to someone's body, sex, and other topics that deal with sexuality, but we must not shy away from the discussion.

Be aware that children progress at different rates emotionally, cognitively, and physically. Varying characteristics of your child's development may follow chronological age (height, weight, physical changes with puberty), while others may trail in cognitive or emotional development. This may help you decide what topics your child can handle in conversation and when.

Certainly, our children and teens need to understand that certain parts of the body are deserving of more respect and privacy. This too is modeled early on in the home when we give them privacy getting dressed or in using the bathroom. We demonstrate it by teaching their siblings to knock before entering a closed door or talking respectfully about the opposite sex. Kids then learn how to treat one another with respect and to also expect others to treat them with respect.

Genesis 5:1–2 says: "When God created mankind, he made them in the likeness of God. He created them male and female and blessed them. And he named them "Mankind" when they were created" (NIV). The Creator of life made male and female, made them in his likeness, and looked back over all he created and called it good. There was no shame and thus no need for covering until sin entered into the world. If a Creator created male and female, sexuality, and sex, then called it good, so must we.

Our kids are growing up in a world that is reshaping their beliefs about these things. If we do not teach them what is right and good and true, who will? They will learn it from somewhere, and as I've mentioned before, it will be all the wrong places.

It's also a safeguard for your child. Children who know and understand how to talk about their body parts and who have been taught privacy and respect for their own bodies and the bodies of others, are more likely to report inappropriate behavior when it happens to them. Professionals and law enforcement officials notice that kids who have been taught these things by their parents are less likely to be abused, are quicker to report when they are, and are better able to articulate what has occurred than other children. This is because they have been given both an understanding of what is healthy and normal, and the language to describe it.[14]

Starting with children as young as age three or four, parents can and should teach their kids about body parts, privacy, and respect for bodies. There are many developmentally appropriate ways to do so: natural conversations when getting dressed or helping in the restroom, incorporating books, stories, and practicing responses to people who may be interacting with them. It involves teaching social skills in how to ask for privacy when using a restroom or changing, when to ask for help, and when to tell a grown-up if something uncomfortable occurs. Kids learn these concepts through simple ideas, pictures, illustrations, and role-playing. These are commonly used strategies to learn about personal space, respect, knowing their body parts, and comprehending privacy.

When one of our boys was four years old, he loved running around the house in his underwear (and sometimes in his birthday suit). He would run out of his room undressed and giggling, saying to everyone, "Look at me!" Then he'd run back into his room. For a toddler, this was innocent, cute, and normal and did not require correction. But imagine if he were thirteen years old and doing that. Not so cute (or appropriate) anymore, right?

How do children learn what is or isn't appropriate? By observing life around them. As a parent, I might smile or laugh at my four-year-old's antics, but then say, "Ok, Buddy, time to get dressed—no one wants to see you running around naked." I am not overreacting or underreacting.

As he gets older, it is important to put reason and rationale to those actions. For example, when you are helping bathe your daughter, you might tell her to wash all areas of her body, including her vagina and behind. It is helpful to talk casually and say, "Honey, remember, no one should ask to see or touch your vagina or behind; those body parts deserve more privacy. Nor should anyone ever ask you to touch their vagina or penis or behind. That's how we show respect—and if anyone ever asks you to do this, please come tell us."

She might respond with, "Mommy, you see me when I am taking a bath."

"Yes," I respond, "There are times Mom and Dad may help you get dressed, dry off from bath-time or help you when you are sick. Doctors may need to look at your body to make sure you are healthy. But if anyone makes you feel uncomfortable, you tell us, and we will talk about it."

Start at a young age when establishing expectations of privacy and respect for others. Every family will have different ways of talking about this: private places or body parts are always covered with clothes or a bathing suit, a person should get undressed in their bedroom or bathroom, who is and isn't allowed to help your child get dressed or use the bathroom. There will be reasons you train your children differently from how another family trains theirs. Your children may require additional help, have greater anxiety (or blind trust), or may be more reserved.

It is important to consider what you know about your own child to help shape how you talk to them. Consider the principles behind the rules you may establish:

- A person's body (yours or others) should be treated with respect.
- Certain parts of the body should be shown greater privacy (be specific and concrete).
- Certain types of affections are reserved for certain people. Discuss what your family guidelines might be.
- If something makes you feel uncomfortable, we want to hear about it.
- You can talk to Mom and Dad about anything.

We often hear that to spot a counterfeit dollar, professionals spend years studying the real thing so that they know every detail of the real dollar bill, therefore, they can spot a fake. To some degree this is how we must think in educating young people. We want them to know God and his ways—what is right and good and healthy—so well that when something inappropriate happens to them, it is clear to them that it is wrong. They may not know of every evil out there, but they can identify something is "off" and seek help.

When Children Are Uncomfortable

Navigating comfortable and uncomfortable touch can feel complicated. Many things are being written today saying we should never force kids to hug or show affection to a relative or any person. The rationale is children should have control of their own bodies and not be forced to show affection. By requiring a hug or kiss, the concern is that we are teaching them to ignore safety signals. The logic for this advice is that children might then think they must comply with any-one's request for affection and this mindset could lead to sexual abuse.

In the field of sexual abuse, there is an understandable hesitancy to force children into displays of affection if it makes them uncomfortable. The argument is that we do not want to teach young people to ignore their feelings and possibly warning signs of danger/grooming. That makes sense. However, for several reasons, I am uncomfortable with this approach (pun intended).

Sometimes kids are uncomfortable because they are asked to do things outside their comfort zone—things that are awkward or hard, but not unsafe. A child who is shy may be uncomfortable when invited to say hello, ask for directions, or talk to a stranger. These are the very things that may save them should they be in peril, but they require the child to step outside their comfort zone. They must learn to do what feels uncomfortable to keep them safe and equipped to get help should they need it.

Other times kids are asked to do things that make them uncomfortable to love others well. It may be to serve the homeless a meal, talk to a Down syndrome individual, or reach out to an elderly person. It may be to help feed them, to make conversation, or offer a hug. Teaching appropriate use and demonstrations of affection is part of equipping our children. The answer is not that kids should never show affection if they are uncomfortable. Rather, the better solution is to teach young people to pay attention to *why* they are uncomfortable.

Take a child who may be uncomfortable hugging grandma. Is it because she is old and smells funny, or does grandma make her sit on her lap and squeeze her too tight? We don't want kids to just ignore their discomfort. Helping kids pay attention to *being* uncomfortable is a valuable tool for assessing safety. But we must then teach them to evaluate *why* they feel uneasy. Here's a sample conversation you could have:

Child: "I don't like hugging grandma."

Parent: "Ok, why don't you like hugging grandma?"

Child: "I don't know. She squeezes me and her kisses are wet."

Parent: "I know, that must make you uncomfortable. Remember how we talked about paying attention to how you feel and trying to figure out why? Do you think grandma is doing anything inappropriate? Why or why not?"

These conversations do not always have an easy answer. Sometimes they do not go smoothly, but they are always helpful. Whenever we stop and try to think about why we feel a certain way, we are becoming more perceptive and discerning. The answer may be simple, or it may be more complicated. It may be innocent, or it may alert us to something amiss.

When I am teaching my children to show affection to anyone, it assumes a certain love of respect and propriety. Love moves us to sometimes do what is uncomfortable, but always safe and good. We want kids to pay attention to these things and then understand the reason why they think or feel the way they do. There might be good and healthy reasons to push through it.

Then there are the uncomfortable feelings that point to something amiss. A hug that lingers too long, a look, stare, or conversation that feels inappropriate or bad to them. We want kids to pay attention to these as well and be able to articulate why. The more you coach them in the day-to-day situations that are often harmless, the more they are prepared for moments that require intervention. You do not want them to learn to minimize what others do to make them uncomfortable; you do want them to learn to discern what the behavior may or may not be about.

Different relationships can be confusing for kids, which is why it's important for parents to be open and candid. Discuss various types of relationships (extended family members, friends, acquaintances, coaches, and teachers) and how these principles apply to these relationships. When is it ok to show affection? If someone asks for a hug, when is it ok to say they are uncomfortable and/or refuse? Give your child options and help them know that you will not be upset if they are uncomfortable.

Here are some examples of what types of affection are appropriate and when:

- Touch that may always be appropriate with anyone: a handshake, pat on the back, fist bump, or high five.
- Affection that may only be appropriate with some: hugs, kisses on the check, etc.
- Affection that never should be expected of them: touching of private parts, undressing, full body hugs.

Practice how to ask friends if it is okay to hug them, how to say no to a request for affection, or how to express if a situation is making them feel uncomfortable. Learning these skills is a significant way to help children discern and prepare for inappropriate versus appropriate interactions and physical contact.

Model the behavior you hope to see in your kids by asking before a hug or a kiss, and asking if you can join them in their room to talk with them. Parents spend much of their time teaching obedience and compliance, but we rarely teach our kids what it looks like to defy or rebuff another person. However, it is an important safety skill. As mentioned earlier, our kids need to hear us say, "If someone ever tells you the right thing to do, you must listen. But if someone, including a grown-up, ever tells you the wrong thing to do, you should never listen. And we will support you."

Accepting and Giving the Answer "No"

We will talk about this more as kids hit the teens and college years, but since so many people are using the language of consent for younger children, let me also weigh in. In simplest terms, consent is giving permission for something to happen, generally in terms of physical touch. It is a term regularly used with children so they learn not to be pressured to do things they do not want to do. It gives them freedom to say yes or no to unwanted touch.

The language of consent teaches kids to respect others and ask permission, and it's most often used in regard to touch and affection.

It really is (or should be) the same language and principles we use when teaching respect—respect for others and their wishes and comfort level, and respect of your own. No one should touch you in ways that are unloving or inappropriate, nor should you ever touch someone in unloving or inappropriate ways. The biblical principle that overarches this is one of love. Paul says in Romans that "love does no wrong to a neighbor" (Romans 13:10). The overarching truth you can teach your children is that God wants them to treat others with respect and likewise no one should be trying to harm them.

Focusing on love not doing harm will help you avoid treating the language of consent as formulaic. That is not what we are looking for. We want to help children learn and practice demonstrations of healthy respect for others and their comfort levels. It is always a good practice to ask for a hug, for permission to help someone, or to move toward someone. It is heathy and wise to teach my kids to have freedom to say when something makes them uncomfortable—even if they realize later on that they had no reason to be. Kids are learning to pay attention to their feelings, and at the same time learning to not live and act based on feelings alone.

Parents can encourage children to accept the word "no" and say "no" in the right setting. It might be with a sibling who is rushing into the bathroom to brush their teeth, on the school playground when another child demands their cell phone, or at a family reunion when a cousin wants them to go somewhere alone, away from the group. Perhaps it is at church when an adult asks for a hug, or with kids in the neighborhood playing truth or dare.

This does not mean a child has ultimate veto power over a parent; rather, it models respectful interaction. Children learn quickly how to work the system, and when given the chance to say no to mom or dad, it may flow from their lips way too easily. Then you know further discussion about obedience versus discomfort is needed. At other times, it may be encouraging to your child that it is okay to say they are not ready to talk or need some space.

This will naturally teach children about asking and giving permission. Teach children to ask permission, whether they are hugging a cousin or borrowing something from someone. Requiring permission underpins the importance of respect and giving others a choice.

Remind them that loving others means we listen when someone tells us, "No," even if we think they are being rude or wrong to do so. When a friend has turned down a request for a hug, parents should encourage their child to accept it. Praise your children when they respond well and respect others' feelings. Sometimes a peer will be rude, even mean, in their response, and it will be necessary to help our kids work through hurt or rejection. In doing so, they learn that how you say no to someone is as important as what you say.

When helping young children to implement good interpersonal habits and build healthy relationships, practice and encouragement is important. Parents should pay attention to how they do (or don't) model privacy respect at home. As a parent, do you always knock before entering their room? Do you model healthy, normal, godly ways of expressing affection as a married couple, and toward your children? Do your kids see you modeling respect when you are with extended family and friends? Much of what our children learn is caught (in watching us), even more than what is directly taught to them.

Affirm young kids when they are showing respect or privacy to another individual. For example, when a sibling is using the bathroom and your son knocks first, or accidentally walks in but quickly apologizes and closes the door, respond with, "I'm so proud that you apologized" or "Good job asking politely to come in while I brush my teeth." What you model is the most practical way of helping kids establish good relationship skills.

Teach young children that "No, thank you" and "Please stop" are important words, and when we hear those words, we show respect.

As mentioned before, the ability to process why a child might say "No" or why they are uncomfortable is essential to building in children the skill of evaluating behavior and becoming discerning. It also gives room to change their minds when they find it safe and wise to do so.

A child who initially says no to a hug because they are in a grumpy mood may feel free to change their mind an hour later when they are feeling more cheerful. A child who says, "That makes me uncomfortable," when an older cousin wants to make them sit together can later process with you why they felt that way, and you can affirm the good decision they made.

Despite our best intentions, parents make mistakes. We miss opportunities for teachable moments. We may even minimize our child's discomfort or dismiss it too quickly. When this happens, simply acknowledge it, apologize, and talk through what you'd do differently. Our kids do not need perfect parents; they need humble ones.

When teaching your kids about what makes them comfortable and asking for permission to show affection, it's important to be aware of the ways in which we unintentionally undermine this. It is easy for parents to fall into the trap of assuming that certain behaviors or expressions of affection are fine, so we brush off our children's discomfort too quickly. "Mr. Holt was just being friendly," we say. Or, "Uncle Joe just squeezes a little tight—it is ok." If extended family members enjoy holding children on their laps and hugging them, but that makes your son or daughter uncomfortable, we should be willing to help them think through how to rebuff unwanted attention.

Parents need to remember to ask and allow a child to express how they feel and why. When appropriate and helpful, allow a child to make decisions about family interactions and to process how they came to that decision. For example, your family is headed to a holiday event where there will be lots of relatives excited to see how the kids have grown and wanting to shower them with affection and attention. You know one of your kids is shy and uncomfortable with this. On your way to the event, you brainstorm with your children what are appropriate displays of affection (to give and to receive), what are not, and how to respond if someone forces affection on them that they do not want. Your daughter says she does not like it when a relative grabs her tight or makes her sit on their lap. You talk through why and affirm that she can greet everyone in ways she is comfortable—like shaking hands, or fist bumps, or a quick hug. Ask what she would prefer and let her know that it is fine to share she doesn't like hugs but will give a handshake.

We do not want our kids to be fearful or uncomfortable with appropriate affection, nor do we want affection to be forced if they need time to feel at ease around others. By failing to allow children the time they need to process, children miss the ability to evaluate both a situation and their feelings. The goal is not always to avoid uncomfortable situations, but to help them understand their own feelings and reactions, then discern how to respond.

Ultimately, all these principles and scenarios point back to how God asks us to live. He asks us to treat others with love and kindness. He made our bodies, so parents must help children realize that their bodies belong to the Lord, and therefore we honor God with our bodies. *That* is the basis for why each of us would allow or not allow affection. Is it right and good and loving, or is it unwise, inappropriate, and unloving? A child cannot always tell, which is why we teach them that when they are uncomfortable, you always want to hear and help them.

Keep Talking

Have the mindset that these conversations with your child will be ongoing. Don't make conversations about sex, safety, privacy, abuse, and the like a one-time event. Children will forget what you've shared without repeated discussion and application. Young people are always growing cognitively, emotionally, and spiritually and processing things in new ways as they develop. What seemed irrelevant to them months ago and was dismissed by them as improbable may now be right before them. What they learned and saw as a toddler may not be challenged until they enter school and have to rebuff someone who is pressuring them. It is vital that we are willing to continue conversations, revisit topics regularly, and welcome—even foster—Q and A for our children. All of this, over time, will add up to discipling your children "along the way" to be discerning and respectful. These conversations will help safeguard them, but more importantly point them to their God—their ultimate safeguard.

CHAPTER 8

Technology and Your Child

"Finally, brothers, whatever is true, whatever is honorable, whatever
is just, whatever is pure, whatever is lovely, whatever is commendable,
if there is any excellence, if there is anything worthy of praise, think
about these things." Philippians 4:8

Media and technology are widely debated topics for many parents.
More often than not, parents give in to the pressure of buying their
kids a variety of electronic devices before their children are prepared
to manage them. Some do so for good reasons (they are home alone
or out at a sporting event and they need to reach a parent) and others do not want their child to feel left out or behind their peers. The
trend of younger and younger children spending time online should
be troubling to us all, yet so many parents are allowing it.

Evaluating Your Technology Decisions

As a parent, it's easy to simply cave into the pressure from your children and the world around you to give your children early access
to technology. But as Christian parents, our first responsibility is to
what God would have us do in this area. The decisions about when
to give your children access to technology and what rules to have
once you do should begin with thinking about Philippians 4:8. This
gives us a different set of questions to ask when we are making these
decisions. What we put into our lives, our hearts, and our minds is
all about what we invest in—is it good, just, right, and honorable?

Will their use of technology be pure, lovely, commendable? Will it help them grow into men and women who love the Lord and steward these things well? Once we start asking these questions, we can gain the perspective we need in a world where young children are being babysat with phones and tablets.

As you think through if your child's use of technology is "commendable," you have to consider what your child is really gaining and losing when they have early, unrestricted access to smart phones, tablets, and other personal electronic devices. What they can lose are important developmental milestones (unstructured play time, development of imagination and creativity, exercise, social interaction), as well as what potential bad habits they may gain (addiction to technology or social media, poor sleep, negatively impacted eating habits, loss of in-person social skills, etc.). What they lose and gain is far more serious than what you and I fear they lose (being ostracized or missing early technology education) or gain (socialization, fitting in with peers, or additional skills). Be sure you are appropriately evaluating the risks and your ability to diminish the risks of your kids being online.

As a parent, would you ever give an eleven or twelve-year-old the keys to your car? Why not? Most would say that would be foolish, maybe illegal, but certainly unwise. The child lacks the resources, skill, maturity, and responsibility to be driving at such a young age. But what if you lived in a town where other parents let their children do so? What if other children were driving around recklessly, and perhaps your child is the only one who is not and feels left out? What if, as a parent, you feel pressure that you are the only parent not allowing your child to drive a car—or you require their driving be supervised and with a great caution? Will you cave to the pressure? Will you hand over the keys of a vehicle that can cause great harm to both your child and others?

This analogy may seem extreme, but I would argue it demonstrates the risks we take by allowing our children access to a device that opens a world full of opportunity and danger before they have the maturity or character to handle it. And the potential risks are disastrous. It is a tall order to expect your children and teens to know all the risks and be mature and wise enough to navigate them on their own.

Make no mistake; people will prey upon your children and find ways to do so. Technology gives a perceived anonymity and boldness to such attempts. Statistics consistently point to the growing numbers of online predatorial behavior. The Child Crime Prevention & Safety Center states that "there are an estimated 500,000 online predators active each day. Children between the ages of 12 and 15 are especially susceptible to be groomed or manipulated by adults they meet online."[15] Through chat rooms, online gaming, messaging and many other avenues, young people are being groomed and sexually solicited—often right under a parent's nose.

Those who wish to harm your children often join the sites and platforms that are popular with young people. They pose as children or teens themselves, strike up a friendship, and send out friend requests. Through sites, apps, online games, and social media, they engage children in an initially harmless conversation to build rapport and a perceived sense of familiarity. Children will feel like they know this person, that they are easy to talk to, and that their online friend "gets" them. Such people gain children's trust so they can slowly separate, isolate, and begin manipulating them.

Safety Guidelines for Technology in the Home

Even if young children do not have their own devices, anyone in your home can potentially gain access to your electronic devices and your internet. Consider some of the following safety guidelines surrounding technology in the home.

It is vital that you have parental controls on all devices, as well as on your internet access. Kids are incredibly savvy at getting around parental controls. Even when kids are not attempting to get around them, there are many apps that allow devious individuals to gain access into your child's world—their gaming devices, apps, and other technology.

There are many good parental controls that you can purchase, download, or that come included on devices. It is important to consider if such controls filter out dangerous content, alert you to suspicious activity or flag certain words, images, or even turn off at pre-prescribed times. New resources are always evolving, so it is necessary to do the research ahead of time. Anticipate what your child may intentionally or unintentionally stumble upon or be tempted to view. Be aware of what makes them vulnerable and who/what may try pursuing them online.

Have an Open Device Policy

This means that all devices will be checked and everyone held accountable for how they use them. The principle is one of accountability, transparency, and good stewardship. We want to teach children stewardship of their devices, as well as self-discipline to put it down and walk away. Until children are old enough and mature or responsible enough to do so, it is a parent's job to monitor this for them.

Everything they post online should be seen as public and accessible, regardless of how strict the privacy setting is on any given app. Help your children understand that it is hard to erase your digital footprint online. You may open a social media account and later decide to delete it, but many people have found ways to dig up the things from years ago that people thought were forever erased. Young people lack the foresight to see that the regretful things they might say or do online today can come back to hurt them weeks, months, and years down the road. It is the responsibility of a parent to help their children learn these lessons before the consequences are too big to rectify.

It is wise to keep all electronics out of a child's bedroom. Numerous studies have shown the impact of kids' sleep when a device is nearby. They are tempted to be on it at all hours of the night, often fostering an addictive habit. Young people are also kept up by the glow and lighting of the screen and the constant chimes of text messages and new notifications. Your son or daughter will say they need the device as an alarm clock, but the easy answer to that is to buy them an alarm clock, rather than allow them to become overly attached to a device.

It is always helpful to have all devices plugged in at night in a centrally located place. Some families do so in the kitchen or family room. Some parents choose to have it their own room so kids will not be tempted to sneak onto the device when no one is around. There are also good parental controls that will automatically shut off the internet. It is generally wise to discourage devices being used in private places (like bathrooms), and instead develop routines where kids know and are expected to use their device in common areas where anyone can view what they are doing. There may be some exceptions, but a fostering openness and accountability is a good practice.

More can be said regarding helpful ways to manage technology, such as a "no technology at mealtime" rule that prevents kids from being on their devices during family meals at home or when at a restaurant. But for the sake of this book, we are focusing on ways to safeguard our children from the perils that technology brings forth.

Far too many parents are accepting that it is "normal" to both allow kids to have devices, as well as assuming their children are prepared for what they will encounter. Be willing to guard your children's hearts for them. They can so easily be harmed or corrupted by the things of this world, and as children they haven't developed the wisdom to know that they are being harmed. You have to hold the line for them.

Regardless of when and how your kids end up on technology, talk to them about prevalent online dangers that exist. Tell them you know things like sexting, cyberbullying, and the like happen, and if they ever feel it is happening to them, you want to know *and will support them*. Over and over, kids need to hear that their parents will not be angry or punitive, but will come alongside their kids and support them as they figure out hard things that are happening or have made unwise choices.

Pornography and Online Images

This leads us to discuss what to do when children are approached online or view things that are inappropriate. The more you have open conversations with your children about dangers like pornography, the more prepared and willing they will be to share with you what they see. Your children need to hear that no topic is off-limits and that you are strong enough to hear anything hard they share.

You can do this by bringing up topics they may be reluctant to discuss. It may be a question like: Have you ever looked at or been sent a picture of someone who is naked? If yes, what was that like? How did it make you feel? If no, what do you think you would do? This leads into a conversation about what you would like them to do: tell mom or dad right away, delete it if it came via text, refuse to give someone a photo of yourself if they ask, etc.

You want to demonstrate to your children that pornography is a safe topic to talk about with you and that what God has to say about these things is vital for them to hear. Even bringing up the topic around the table while having dinner helps model that you as a family are comfortable with talking about these things. You are modeling that you know such things exist and are not afraid of the subject matter. Be the first one to say, "You may see images of people who are naked or doing inappropriate things in a picture. It may surprise you, confuse you, or make you feel curious. We want you to come and tell us so we can help you know what to do." This is not a script you follow, but a mindset to have so your kids will know you expect it and can handle such events. It is trying to normalize the reality that bad things are out there in the world, and you are there to help them navigate it.

Here is where knowing your children's tendencies is important. One of our children was highly sensitive to images, whether it was inappropriate or scary. His response was to cover his eyes until the image disappeared. Another one of our children was transfixed by imagery and would lean in with utter curiosity. Both responses tell us something about our children's weaknesses and ways of responding. Clues like this will help shape the way you parent different children.

Here are some ways you can consider setting up healthy guardrails to protect children online:

- Establish early on the principles of stewardship and accountability. You want your family to learn to steward their lives well. All they have, including access to technology and electronic devices, is both a privilege and responsibility. With such responsibility comes accountability and an expectation of their willingness to be transparent and accountable for how they manage what they are given.

- Always have parental controls for family devices. Regardless of the rules you establish for your home, it is important to have guardrails set up for your kids. Parental controls give families the ability to filter out graphic and unwanted content, allow you to manage the amount of time children are on various sites, games, or shopping, and can shut off when time limits are reached. Parental controls help provide a natural accountability and lessons for stewardship without you policing and fighting to gain access to their devices.

- Consider why you allow kids to have certain social media accounts, platforms, or online access. Do they really need it? Is it a necessary way of communicating with clubs, schools, or youth groups? What are the pros, cons, dangers, and benefits?

- Consider healthy lifestyle standards you want to help young people establish. Be proactive in preventing kids from staying on devices all hours of the night, creating habits for a good night's sleep, and setting up standards that keep devices out of bedrooms and used in common areas.

- What is needed from one child to the next may vary. It is important to know basic guiding principles and rules for your home, and when you want to adapt rules because it makes sense to do so for the needs of an individual or for a season.

- When helping young people decide how to navigate being on devices, train them to avoid putting personal information online. Describe what information might be safe to post (first name, age, grade), and what is unwise to post (last name, address, phone numbers, where they attend school, etc.). Helping them understand how that information could be misused helps them begin to discern if what they are about to say is wise or unwise. Should they ever announce they are home alone? Is it wise to announce you will be going on vacation (and the house will be empty)?

- Explain that expressing or venting your feelings online is not only unwise but can have grave consequences. In a moment of anger, harsh things can be said that cause a chain reaction.
- Talk at length about what is inappropriate online, such as inappropriate images or comments, as well as sexually explicit conversations, and encourage them to tell you or another trusted adult if they are either intentionally or unintentionally exposed to such content. Teach them never to respond or send a picture. Remind them you always want to know if they've gotten into something like this and that they will never be in trouble for telling you. If kids feel they will be blamed, it causes them to hide what they are seeing and prevents you from helping them respond.
- Be an online presence as well. You should always be a friend or connection on any sites your kids are on so you can see how they present themselves and can continue to disciple your kids as they form their own identity. You also can observe what others are saying and posting on your child's accounts. This will help you be aware of any bullying or negative interactions sooner than later.

This might sound like an overwhelming amount of work to do (and it is a lot of work!). But remember that your overarching goal is to raise your children to know right and wrong and to want to walk in the right direction. Doing the hard work God has called you to do will help keep your children safe. I have counseled many parents who were filled with regret over not doing the hard work and taking the appropriate steps to safeguard their children. Thankfully we know God can use our mistakes and failure. It is *never too late* to take these steps. It may be harder to undo bad habits, it may take more effort and persuasion, but it will always be worth it. How much better would it be to begin proactively working to safeguard your children. But while you do that hard work with them, don't forget to always remind them that God is our ultimate defense.

CHAPTER 9

When Children Bully or Are Bullied

"Be kind to one another, tenderhearted, forgiving one another, as
God in Christ forgave you." Ephesians 4:32

The apostle Paul sets a high standard for us and our children for
how we should treat one another—we are called to be kind, tenderhearted, and forgiving—like Jesus. A model of biblical kindness is
one that seeks to serve, cares about the needs of others, builds them
up, and speaks in charitable ways, regardless of personal differences.
Remember, to evaluate behavior, our kids must be taught what is
right and good. Even more significantly, our kids need us to live this
out before them. Ephesians 4:32 can set the standard in your home
for how you and your children treat family members, friends, and
acquaintances. Have your children memorize it and use it frequently
as a family. It will be a helpful guide for so many situations children
find themselves in, but it directly applies to bullying behaviors that
your child might experience or even participate in.

When teaching our children about bullying behaviors, it is
important that they are able to identify what kindness looks like. That
may seem obvious, but our children are growing up in an increasingly
uncharitable culture. We feel justified in being rude, blunt, harsh,
and bold in our opinions and comments—especially online or in the
public forum. We feel we have a right (maybe even responsibility)
to be outraged and abrasive in our responses to people who do not

share our firmly held opinions. Children are watching and becoming equally unsympathetic.

Not only is it possible for your child to be the target of bullying, it is also possible they will succumb to bullying behaviors. Whether it is due to peer pressure, personal frustration, a desire to get even, or hoping to fit in with the wrong group, children can find themselves participating in the mistreatment of their peers. It is hard for a parent to imagine their child would be the perpetrator of bullying, but it can take on many forms. Kids may not even consider what they are doing to be bullying. Bully behaviors can include things like threatening actions, mocking or ridiculing, or intimidating or coercing others to do your will.

Chances are, you have even experienced this yourself. Someone has said hurtful things to you in person, through text, or online. Perhaps they have tried to discredit you or the work you do. Whether it's a neighbor, colleague at work, or a stranger on the internet, criticism of your faith or political views, we all have faced unkindness. We all need to learn how to respond to or even sometimes ignore unkindness. The question is, when does unkindness turn to cruel or bullying patterns? Bullying, especially of our kids, should not be ignored. Children may be targeted and mistreated by those who are older, stronger, or more aggressive. Addressing the issue of bullying means understanding why your child may be vulnerable to bullying or why they may become bullies.

Bullying Trends

Both boys and girls bully. Boys bully more often and are more likely to experience physical bullying. Girls are more likely to experience emotional bullying and sexual provocation. Behaviors that fall into bullying can seem like "normal" unkind acts—perhaps ones you might even encourage your child to overlook. However, what makes them more serious is they are often repeated and habitually cruel actions. Another criterion is the perception (by the bully or others) of an imbalance of power or position. This is what makes it different from conflict that requires kids to learn to work things out versus mistreatment that requires intervention. Those who are seen as being weak, smaller, unpopular, unattractive, or different from their peers are more likely to be mistreated. And those that are mistreating others are likely seen as stronger, more powerful or influential, more popular, older, and can punish or harm.

Kids may also be targeted due to a temperament that appears timid, passive, fearful, or unassertive. Understanding this helps parents be proactive and teach skills to their child so he or she knows how to speak up and be assertive when the moment requires. Role-playing and practice are so important here because you are trying to help your child become comfortable doing something that feels unnatural for them. In order to stand up for what is right or get help, they need to practice both what to do and say.

The most common ways we see bullying manifested are the following:

- Physical: pushing, hitting, kicking, and tripping
- Verbal: mocking, name-calling, ridiculing, or belittling
- Social: ostracizing peers, spreading lies or rumors, or spreading embarrassing images or information about another peer
- Damage to property: breaking backpacks, throwing away lunches, taking devices and smashing them, stealing from peers

Bullying has evolved from the typical playground scenario where kids are picked on, to cyberbullying. Cyberbullying or cyberharassment is a form of bullying or harassment using electronic means. It is also called online bullying. It has become increasingly common, especially among teenagers, as the digital sphere has expanded, and technology has advanced. Cyberbullying is when someone (typically a teenager) harasses or threatens others on the internet. Bullying is harmful to young people regardless, but with online bullying the impact goes beyond the school yard and into homes. It pervades kids' lives in ways that feel inescapable.

If your child is targeted for harassment online, don't assume he or she will tell you what is going on. Many kids hide it from their parents. Please don't wait to speak into these issues until you suspect something might be happening. If you are not talking to your children about this problem, they will be left to figure out how to respond on their own, and the results can be devastating. For many teens, bullying leads to feelings of despair and hopelessness, and they often look for unhealthy ways to cope, including: giving into the demands, trying to appease, fighting back with similar behaviors, or giving up and contemplating suicide because they can see no other way out.

Practical Steps to Address Bullying

Fostering conversation is essential. Teaching children kindness and respect as a lifestyle is vital. Notice when others are modeling this and point it out to your children. Encourage them to notice when others are not and use it as a teachable moment to discuss what could or should be done. Even minor acts of rudeness and teasing should be evaluated. Help kids be more aware of how and when someone could be hurt, even by joking and teasing.

Teach your children how to be assertive in all the right ways. Encourage your children to share their feelings clearly, have freedom to say when they feel uncomfortable or pressured, and allow them to stand up for themselves. Give them options for how to walk away from concerning or dangerous situations. They will not always get things right or read a situation correctly, but that is why practice and discussion are so valuable, so they can learn to think things through and become wise and discerning.

It's important to be someone who is willing to intervene when you see mistreatment. When our kids see us standing up for the vulnerable, they are observing and learning godly ways to stand up for those who need help. For example, if you step in to aid an elderly man who is being mistreated by teens in a store parking lot, you are modeling courage and compassion to your children. They are also learning how others should respond to them. When you tell an older child on the playground that is unkind and rude not to speak to their peer harshly, you are modeling how to respond to mistreatment. Encourage your children to stand up against mistreatment when they see it. Talk about who to go to, role-play with them how to talk to a bully, and when to inform a teacher and what to do if the bullying doesn't stop.

Scripture is full of pleas for God's people to defend those who are weaker or more vulnerable: "Open your mouth for the mute, for the rights of all who are destitute. Open your mouth, judge righteously, defend the rights of the poor and needy" (Proverbs 31:8–9) and "Learn to do good, seek justice, correct oppression . . . " (Isaiah 1:17).

We are given stories in Scripture like that of the Good Samaritan (Luke 10:30–37) who stepped in to care for someone who had been mistreated and beaten. Compassion and courage are taught and modeled when we move toward the needs of others.

Listen to and help children who tell you others are mistreating them. Telling a parent about bullying is not easy for a child or teen. If a child comes to you seeking assistance with bullying, spend time listening to them and helping them process what they are experiencing. You can help a child gather ideas on how to respond, be a support to them behind the scenes, and discuss when it is important for someone to intervene on their behalf. Knowing they are not in it alone can help kids feel competent to take steps and be assertive when necessary.

Parents have varying rules and ideas about when and how to defend oneself against a bully. Be concrete and practical about what your child can or cannot do in defending themselves (fighting back, walking away, intervening for sibling or peer, finding an adult to help them). Help them consider how and when they would choose to respond to bullying.

You also must clearly communicate expectations and consequences. Your children are less likely to participate in bullying or to allow it if expectations and consequences are clear. When children and adults alike are willing to stop bullying behaviors, we change the environment around us. Deliver a clear message to your children that you expect them to show respect and kindness.

You also should feel confident in expressing to your school or day care provider that your child's well-being is your utmost priority, and you want to be made aware of any bullying behaviors that involve or impact your child personally.

Face-to-face bullying and online bullying often happen in conjunction with each other. But cyberbullying leaves a digital trail that can provide evidence to help stop the mistreatment. Knowing this helps kids to take steps to inform adults who can assist them in putting an end to the harm. Parents can and should teach kids how to navigate the perils and possibilities that come from online activity.

Tips for Teaching Kids to Respond to Cyberbullying or Inappropriate Conduct Online

- Decide who can see your social media profile(s), send you direct messages, or comment on your posts by setting up account privacy settings.
- Discuss when to report lies or false information. Does it harm another human being? Is it spreading misinformation that can cause damage to someone's reputation?
- Report to any caring authority (teacher, administrator, parent, coach, etc.) anyone who is posting naked, inappropriate, or embarrassing photos or videos of someone on social media.
- Never send, laugh at, join in, or condone hurtful, abusive, or threatening messages, images, or videos via messaging platforms.
- Report hurtful comments, messages, photos, and videos, and request they be removed from a social media platform.
- Besides "unfriending," you can completely block people to stop them from seeing your profile or contacting you.
- You are in control and responsible for your accounts, regardless of what others may try to comment on. You can and

should choose what comments you want to be seen on your social media. You can delete posts on your profile or hide them from individuals as needed.

Many kids fear typecasting or being labeled a snitch or tattletale. Such labels prevent kids from seeing what is really happening (mistreatment or wrongdoing), and instead put them on the defensive. Helping kids understand that others might label them a snitch (but that's only because they want to silence them), gives them a reason to speak up and speak out against bullying wherever they see or experience it.

A guiding principle as your kids navigate all of this is Ephesians 5:11–12, "Take no part in the worthless deeds of evil and darkness; instead, expose them. It is shameful even to talk about the things that ungodly people do in secret" (NLT). Set the standard for the kindness of Christ for your kids and empower them to take a stand against what is wrong and immoral.

CHAPTER 10

Equipping Children in Case They Get Lost

"When I am afraid,
I put my trust in you." Psalm 56:3

Should a child ever get lost, the most natural thing for them to do is panic. When kids panic, they often do not think clearly and might freeze. This leaves them distraught or, even worse, vulnerable to being approached by the wrong person. This is why role-play and practice are so important. It is natural for children to panic in a fearful moment, but the more practice and repetition they have of potential situations, the more likely they are to remember what they've learned and put it into practice. Done well, this will not build fear in children, but will instead give them confidence and competence.

Instill in them that wherever they go, God goes before them and with them. Build in your children the truth that they are never truly alone and "God is a very present help" in time of trouble (Psalm 46:1). Then, talk through ways God can be a help and comfort to them in the trouble of being lost: They can pray for help; they can recite a passage they have memorized; they can ask for wisdom and God will give it generously. You can help them memorize a short verse like Psalm 56:3 that they can remember when they are afraid that will help them not panic and think about what you have taught them to do next.

Then you can take some simple steps that will help them know what to do in case they do get lost. In most places we took our children when they were young, I would stop and say, "If you were to get separated from me, where would be a good place to meet so I can find you?" If we were at the mall, I'd help them pick a large water fountain, or the mall carousel or an easily found meeting place. If we were at a park, I might tell them to go to the slide at the playground, or stand outside the public restrooms, etc. Help them brainstorm an assigned meeting place. The more invested they are in the decision, the more likely they are to remember.

Who to Go to for Help

Next, help your children to know who to go to for help. As a parent, you could have many options: have them look for another parent, a woman, a security officer, a mall employee, etc. Though there are many ways to approach it, let me persuade you why some will be more helpful than others. For example, when a child is lost, if you were to tell them to go find a police officer, how often will an officer be accessible, or even nearby? For young children, anyone dressed in a uniform (even the janitor) may look like an officer.

One approach I used with my children while they were growing up was to tell them to go find a mom with kids. Why? There are several reasons: First, having a child choose whom they go to prevents panic and fear setting in. They'll immediately know what to do. Helping them know who they will approach also prevents them from being approached by an unwanted (and potentially unsafe) adult. Wherever they go, giving them the skills to know what to do, who to go to and what to say, is always going to build confidence. The moment they are lost, they know to go look for a mom who has children.

Second, a mother with children will likely feel maternal protective instincts for a lost child. If my child were to be lost, I would certainly want someone with maternal instincts to protect my child until I am reunited with them. Third, more often than not, the large majority of offenders are male. Although there are female offenders (who are equally dangerous), the chances of my child picking one out to approach, who has children with them, is decreased.

What to Say

Often, we take for granted that children know how to ask for help. Many children, however, do not even know their parents' first names or phone numbers. Some young people overshare online and may give out too much information. Here is where helping kids understand that dissimilar situations require varying responses is important. Kids playing online video games should never give out a phone number, address, or personal info when asked. Kids lost in a store should be encouraged and equipped to give out a phone number, share their name or their parent's name, or know how to reach someone.

Basic information every child should know:

- Mom and Dad's first and last name
- Their parents' phone numbers (most kids press a button on their phone for mom or dad, but it prevents kids from being prepared when they are without their own device)
- Their address, name of their school, what church they attend, a teacher's full name (this is helpful should they get separated at a school event or field trip, or at a church event or trip)

Kids can be prepared ahead of time for special events, like a school trip, church retreat, concert, etc. It requires taking the basic information they have learned and helping them apply it to the current context. Some parents may place an index card with important information about the child—grade, teacher's name, school, and a phone number, then place it in a child's coat pocket. Rather than memorizing new info all the time, this helps a child know what information to give, or allows them to simply pull it out of their pocket should they need help.

For example, your young teen is going to a concert with a group of peers and another parent. He is excited to go to a concert, hang out with his friends, and is oblivious to the thought that he could find himself in need of help. You want him to be excited and unafraid, but you also want him to be prepared should he need help.

You prep him with the full name of the adults who will be present. Perhaps you have him record it in his phone, along with their phone number. Maybe you know he will be close to his aunt and uncle's home, so you also include their full names and phone numbers should he need to contact a relative close by. For kids without devices, again, you can write details down on an index card that can be slipped into a pocket.

In the case of a concert, you'd rather have your child be able to immediately reach the adult with them or one nearby, then only finding a way to reach you and then you reach the parent. You are trying to give him the simplest way to get immediate help and be reunited with his group.

Identify a Meeting Place

If I were the adult taking a group of kids, I would stop them at the venue and identify an easily recognized meeting place to go should they get separated from the group. Identifying a meeting place in case people get separated is a great practice to get into with your family. No one plans for it to happen, but everyone is thankful for this safety plan when they are lost.

Many years ago, we took our kids to an amusement park. As the day came to a close, our youngest son was tired, so I took him back to the hotel while my husband stayed with the older kids to continue the fun. While sitting at the hotel, it struck me that we had not reviewed our normal routine of "Where do we meet if we get separated? Who do you go to? What is our name and phone number?" I shrugged it off and thought little of it, *until* they walked through the door, crying, upset, and complaining, with my husband following and shaking his head with frustration.

Trying to negotiate multiple kids who wanted to go on different rides, he made sure several kids were in line for one ride and then took another child to another ride nearby. He told the kids he would be standing between the two rides waiting for all to get off and he got in place so he could see both exits to the rides.

Meanwhile, two kids decided they no longer wanted to stay in line and preferred to join their sibling on the other ride. They got out of one line and went looking for the next ride. It was now dark, lights flashing all over the amusement park, roller coasters going on behind them and it was loud. They became disoriented and could not find the beginning of the ride. They also could not find their way back to where my husband was waiting.

By the time both rides were over, he was short two children who were nowhere to be found. When he did find them, who did they go to when they were lost? A group of teenagers! Not only was this not what we trained them to do, but almost the last choice I'd want them to make. It was a perfect moment to put into practice all they had been taught, and it failed.

Here were four children whose parents had gone to great lengths to educate them on what to do and who to look for if lost. We had role-played and practiced with them. Yet, when the time came to put it into practice, things did not go as planned.

Why did none of the training we gave them seem to kick in? First, most children who feel safe and secure never really think they'll need the skills they've been given. Our children had never previously been lost nor had reason to practice in real life the things we had taught them. It is easy to lull oneself into thinking, "It will never happen to me," until it does.

Second, when we find ourselves in fearful situations, many of us tend to panic or freeze. We become disoriented and forget what to do, even if for a brief period. This is why practice and role-playing are so crucial. The more one does it, the more likely they are to remember those skills when needed. Third, many kids feel more comfortable going to those who feel easiest to approach and those they personally may look up to. For our kids, that was a group of teenagers who looked and acted mature (in their minds, at least).

The one time I did not start the experience off with the typical, "Ok guys, where would we meet if we got separated, and who would you go to if you got lost?" is the one time they could have used the reminder. Although it would appear that all our role-playing and practice did not work, I'd argue it is a great example of why we need the practice and reminders. Most kids will not remember what to do in a moment of panic. However, the more one practices what to do, the more likely all skills and instincts will kick in and begin to inform how to get through a precarious situation.

The Lord: Our Ultimate Helper

We can do everything possible to prepare our children for the trials they will face, and then we must place them in the Lord's hands. How comforting it is that we can rely on our God, who always knows where we are and what we need. As much as we dread our children facing potential danger and the possibility they will not handle it well, I am also reminded that God goes before them and will be their helper. Remind your children of this as often as you remind them of what to do when they get lost.

CHAPTER 11

Wisdom Issues: Sleepovers

"If any of you lacks wisdom, let him ask God, who gives generously to
all without reproach, and it will be given him." James 1:5

At its essence, this book is about growing in wisdom in how to safeguard our children from a dangerous world. There are some issues that
different families will come up with different answers to, based on
their situation, needs, and even personalities and preferences. These
next three chapters are meant to help parents think through how to
make wise decisions in the areas of sleepovers, family safe words, and
a family safety plan. The amount of information might seem overwhelming, but as you read, remember that they are suggestions,
options, and at times principles for how to approach each subject. The
Lord gives wisdom to those who ask and you have freedom to decide
how it applies to your family and your particular needs.

Differing Viewpoints on Sleepovers

Of your many parenting decisions, sleepovers can be one that is particularly controversial for parents, and you are likely to have a strong
opinion based on your own personal experience. Some parents are
opposed to sleepovers, stating that the risks far outweigh the benefits.
Other parents have very fond, positive memories of sleepovers and feel
they can adequately prepare and guarantee safety in another home.

Early on, my husband and I made the decision to avoid sleepovers. As a counselor, I knew far too much about the potential pitfalls and how common the risks and problems are at a sleepover. However, this is a wisdom guideline for us more than an unbending rule. Let me explain. There were homes that we could feel as confident as one could feel about allowing our kids to safely spend the night. Although as a rule of thumb we wanted to avoid sleepovers, we did want the ability to make exceptions as our children got older and circumstances proved safe to do so. It may be rare, but we wanted to be open to the possibility. For example, there might be times where a long night out or trip required getting in very late. Did it make sense to drive further out of the way to return a child home or was it reasonable to say our child could spend the night and we would be there early in the morning to get them? Did we trust the parent enough, ask the right questions, and have enough confidence that the risks were minimum, and the benefits made sense?

We knew there would inevitably be special circumstances where we would need to rely on safe homes for our children to spend the night, whether it was because we had to go out of town or we had other situations that required leaning on another family to help care for our children. So, we needed to have preestablished homes where we knew we could trust appropriate safety measures to be taken. You may decide that you will only allow sleepovers with relatives, cousins, or close family members. However, the same risks and cautions must be applied, despite how well you think you know another family.

Some may argue that this selective approach creates too much confusion or can cause hard feelings with people. Yes, the risk is there, yes, it would be easier to have a firm rule, and yes, we have had a few moments of uncomfortable conversation, but we were willing to do so when an exception made sense. And by the way, there were very few of those exceptions. It can be confusing for your kids as they get older to know they were allowed to spend the night at one home, but not another. Yet, if you are thoughtful about why you do what you do, you are helping your kids gain something far better than a hard and fast rule; they are learning to be wise and discerning.

Careful conversations about why we made those choices were always needed, and those conversations were helpful for our whole family. We found our kids could find flaws in our thinking that were good for us to admit and consider. We also modeled to our kids that we were not making our decision about sleepovers like it was a moral right or wrong, as much as a wisdom issue and personal family conviction.

What about allowing sleepovers in your home? Is it confusing or a double standard to allow your children to invite kids over for a sleepover, but not allow them to go to their friend's house? Many parents would say yes. It is a fair point to consider. Again, it is a wisdom issue. Can you guarantee safety and supervision in your home? Can you be confident that the kids you allow to sleepover with follow your rules, even when unsupervised? How will you handle devices they bring with them into the home, and will their parents support the rules you have about where technology must stay when in your home? Many of these are good questions to consider even when your children's friends are simply visiting.

As a family, we often open our home for ministry. We served as a foster family, which meant kids were coming and going in our home. We did have individuals live with us for a season, and with that came risks we always had to evaluate. We also wanted our kids to learn the value of hospitality and inviting in those in need. Occasionally for us, that did mean allowing a child to spend the night. Perhaps this seems like a side issue, or irrelevant to making decisions for sleepovers, but it is not. Similar concerns, questions, and risks must be evaluated. As a family who chooses to invite hard and challenging ministry situations into our home, wisdom will still be needed and evaluating the safety of our home is still important. Your family may choose to serve in ways that are outside your home and do not require these considerations. You may choose to have an open-door policy and want your children to have friends and people visit regularly. Regardless, you can see how wisdom should and will be the guide in such circumstances.

Evaluating Safety Concerns for Sleepovers

Let's talk through the safety concerns when it comes to having sleepovers, either in your home or sending your kids to a friend's house. These considerations will help you make wise, informed, careful decisions.

The most obvious threat that might occur at a sleepover is that of sexual vulnerability or sexual abuse. As a counselor, I can speak to the validity of this concern. Sadly, many times I have had to help families walk through the aftermath of the molestation of their child at a sleepover. Often this occurred in homes that they thought would be safe. Why is this?

There may be several factors to consider. To start, families have varying levels of supervision and rules. One family may consider it a normal practice to have siblings sleep in each other's rooms, while another may not. A parent may be comfortable allowing their teenager to be in charge during a sleepover while they run an errand or go out for a few hours. Some parents may consider good supervision consists of being home and present, but the kids are spending most of their time in a basement level family room away from the view of parents, playing video games, or surfing online. Other parents may be comfortable with their children running to and from neighbors homes, so they allow your children to as well, or invite neighborhood kids to come join their children while yours are visiting.

Even if you ask all the right questions (and you should!), there are so many various unforeseen circumstances you cannot plan for (the unexpected guest, the friend of a sibling who stops over, the change in sleeping arrangements, who will be allowed access to your child, what to do if your child wakes up in the middle of the night scared and wants to come home, what rules they have about TV or movies, etc.).

There can be many "what if" situations, so it is important to consider what questions you must ask and what you need to know before you feel comfortable with even a drop-off play date, and what are the additional questions you have to allow for an overnight sleepover.

You can know families with shared beliefs and values, but the way those principles are lived out may look very different. For example, one family may also believe it is very important to limit technology use and have parental controls on. So, you assume that when your child spends the night, there will be close supervision. However, when your child returns home, they report staying up all night watching horror movies, or you find out they spent three hours watching online videos while the parents were upstairs.

Technology makes every scenario more complicated. In other families' homes kids often can gain access to electronic devices all hours of the night. Parents may not allow kids to be on a computer, but what happens when parents fall asleep and kids are still up at midnight and bored? If a home does not have parental controls and technology blocked, children can and often do look for ways to surf the internet and watch videos, or even view scary or inappropriate things on TV.

The risks to consider are significant: an older sibling having a device that has access to pornography, an adult in the home with unlocked devices, televisions in children's rooms, and more. It becomes exhausting to even try to establish what level of supervision or control every home has over such things. Many families have no parental controls on devices and few rules that are well enforced. Perhaps they do have very good rules, but their kids are savvy enough to get around parental controls.

A family's comfort level with appropriate or inappropriate language, music, and movies, or their comfort level with the presence of kids from their neighborhood all require a great deal of trust that a family shares the same values, expectations, and concerns that you do. Just because someone is being raised in a moral or Christian family does not mean you can assume that their standards of conduct are the same. You cannot assume everyone who comes to their home or who is living in their home is of the same mindset or has the same values they do.

From scary movies, to pornography, chat rooms, truth or dare, to risky, reckless behaviors, sleepovers provide a greater opportunity for such situations because of the longer overnight time frame and because much of that time is often spent away from a parent's view. Any time our kids are visiting another home, it is wise to ask good questions, but it is also unrealistic to demand that another family conform to your standards (regardless of how good you think they are). Instead, you should evaluate and make choices based on what you do know and sometimes what you don't know (who will be present, what they are like, what access to technology will they have, etc.).

We cannot demand that another family conform to all our standards, but we can and should ask questions that help us decide if we are comfortable with our children in their home. Below are some suggestions of things to ask before your child spends time at another home:

- Who lives in the home? Who will be present while your child is there?
- What are the guidelines or rules regarding technology, movies, TV, and how it is enforced?
- Are their older siblings in the home? Are they ever left in charge?
- Will you be going anywhere with my child? Who will be driving?
- Do you have guns in your home? Are they secure?
- Will your child be around anyone who smokes, vapes, or uses drugs?
- How do you handle behavior issues?
- What will the sleeping arrangements be?

Requests you may have for your own children may be things like:

- I would like my child to be free to call me whenever they ask.
- I am comfortable/not comfortable with my child using _____ _____ (technology, games, viewing certain shows or movies).

- My son or daughter has food/animal allergies. Will this be an issue?
- Please contact me should my child need discipline.
- Who is permitted to help young children needing help dressing, using the restroom, etc.?

If this all sounds arduous to you, it's because it is! But don't let embarrassment, the dread of uncomfortable conversations, or fatigue stop you from asking the questions that will help protect your children from unsafe situations. All of these concerns are what led us to make a general guideline that we don't usually allow sleep overs. "Love does no harm to a neighbor" also applies to our own children—we don't want any harm to come to them, so we make choices to keep them out of harm's way (Romans 13:10).

CHAPTER 12

Wisdom Issues: Childcare Guidelines

"If any of you lacks wisdom, let him ask God, who gives generously to all without reproach, and it will be given him." James 1:5

Another issue that requires asking God for wisdom (and trusting that he will supply) is deciding on childcare for your children. Looking for a babysitter or childcare provider can be a daunting mission as a parent. Some feel confident in the babysitter or childcare provider they have. They have known the individual for years, the sitter is familiar with your rules and expectations, and the parents are confident they would know if something were amiss.

Having someone who has watched our kids and knows our routines, rules, and expectations is a gift. It can also lull us into a false sense of confidence. That self-confidence may cause us to skip asking good questions or prevent us from looking for important warning signs. Familiarity can be comforting, but it can also be potentially blinding.

Other parents may struggle with worry and vague insecurity when leaving their children at a childcare program or with someone new. They hope their child is safe and is being well cared for, yet they live with a generalized fear that perpetually leaves them anxious without a way of alleviating their worry. This generalized hypervigilance and anxiety certainly is not constructive, and it is too ambiguous to give any real insight on potential problems. When we do not know what to look for or how to interview a potential childcare provider, it will hinder us from making confident choices.

Discerning the Right Questions to Ask

When our children were younger, we struggled with childcare decisions and with knowing who might be a good fit. We served as foster parents and knew that whoever babysat for us needed a level of knowledge and skill that might not be needed for other families. We also were conscientious that the needs of the children in our home could vary at any given time. We also had strong personalities to parent. Knowing this helped shape the kind of questions we asked when interviewing possible candidates. You too will have unique needs and circumstances in your family, and, like us, you will need to think carefully about what they are and ask God for wisdom on what questions to ask and what needs to prioritize.

On one occasion, we interviewed a potential babysitter. We got to know her, asked background questions, and then jumped into how she would handle various situations. Knowing we had four young, active kids and that our crew could be a handful, our natural question was: "How would you handle misbehavior in one of our children?" Her answer was, "Oh, I am sure they would never do anything bad. I would just love on them, and I know they'll be good kids for me. I am sure they will always be good." My immediate thought was, "My children are going to eat you alive." Needless to say, we did not hire her. As delightful as she was, we needed someone who both understood the nature of rambunctious children and had the ability to manage poor behavior as needed.

I am repeatedly surprised by how little parents do to interview either a babysitter, childcare facility, or school. We ask basic logistic questions: How much do you charge? When can you work? What is the schedule like? What are pick up or drop off times? We often hesitate, however, to ask the harder questions: What are your rules regarding discipline? Have you ever worked with a child you thought was being abused? How have you handled emergencies? How will you keep us informed and what will prompt you to call a parent?

Especially when it comes to school and childcare programs, we tend to put a blind confidence in the fact that an established institution equates a certain level of credibility. That may or may not be accurate. Rarely do families ask to see licenses, discipline policies, or how an institution will support their goals for their children.

Since there are countless options when it comes to childcare, babysitters, and nannies, it is important that you both know what to ask, what to look for, and what to watch for once you've made a decision. Before you choose, it's important to consider these questions to inform your decision:

1. Given my family and my children's needs, what am I looking for in a childcare provider?
2. What things will I specifically need a childcare provider to do or be skilled at?
3. What are my expectations of a childcare provider, and can they fill the role?
4. What will determine whether I can trust or have confidence in this person?
5. What kind of values will they be instilling in my children, whether caught or taught?
6. How will I evaluate how the babysitter (or my children) are doing?
7. What qualifications do I want a sitter to have? Is it important they have first aid and CPR training and/or extensive babysitting experience?
8. Aside from babysitting, what else will I be asking them to do, such as clean, make dinner, or pick the kids up from school?

Once you have considered what your needs are, compile a list of interview questions. The following is a sample of things you might ask a potential babysitter and what their responses might tell you about this person:

1. What do you like about working with children? What do you dislike? Listen for how natural, comfortable, and engaging they appear with kids.

2. Are you comfortable giving me three references and doing a background check? It is a red flag when someone is hesitant to do so.

3. How many families have you babysat for? How many children have you watched in a home? If they don't have any experience, some parents may find that preferable so they can more easily train someone to work with their individual family needs. Some may find lack of experience as a detriment.

4. What behaviors annoy you? Pay attention to the answer, but follow up with, "How do you handle those behaviors?"

5. How would you discipline a child? This will give insight into how strict, lenient, or unprepared they are for discipline issues. It also provides a context to share how you would like your children to be handled when discipline is needed.

6. Have you ever dealt with an emergency? Tell me about it and how you dealt with it. If they struggle to come up with a situation, share some possible issues they could face with your children and ask them to tell you how they would respond.

7. Are you comfortable bathing, helping dress, or changing a child who has an accident? This allows you to talk about the guidelines you have in your home and how you expect them to treat your child when it comes to issues of privacy and respect for their bodies. It also puts the issue of abuse on the table, should you want to express that you take seriously any risk to your child and expect them to as well.

8. What activities do you do with children? As a parent, you want to know how engaged and nurturing they will be with your kids. Do they have creative ideas, enjoy walks and trips to the park, or would they stick your children in front of screens? It is good to talk about your expectations.

9. Are you comfortable staying off your phone, or keeping it plugged in one room? As a parent, it is important you have someone whose attention is undivided while babysitting. Establish

ground rules for how you'd like them to handle technology for both themselves and your children. It also is an opportunity to discuss your rules about inviting people over or being online with friends while babysitting.

10. Tell us about past babysitting jobs. What went well, and what did not? What other jobs you have had? What did you like or dislike about them?

11. Have you ever suspected a child was being abused? How did you handle it if so, or how would you handle it if such a concern arose? Though it is equally valid to ask a babysitter if they have ever abused a child, most parents feel uncomfortable asking such a blunt question. This allows you to get a sense of how this person handles the topic and it puts it out there as an issue you are willing to face.

12. How do you handle disobedience and discipline? You want to discern both how they handle discipline and how they would speak to your kids about their behavior or encourage good behavior.

13. Have you had situations where you disagreed with a parent (and/or their rules)? How did you handle it?

14. What will you do if my children won't get along with each other? It's always helpful to see how they handle conflict.

Nanny Cameras and Video Recording

Do you ever wonder if having a nanny camera in your home will protect your children? Is it helpful to have cameras running regularly to observe what is happening when you aren't home?

Many parents do not want to be suspicious of those they have entrusted to care for their children. They choose to trust that either the sitter is competent and providing good care, or that their children would alert them if anything were amiss. They do not like the idea of snooping on their babysitters and they believe they have no reason to.

Other parents may feel a sense of hesitancy. Perhaps you have always had a bit of a concern about your childcare provider, but you never could quite put your finger on why. Maybe you are a worrier and wonder what happens when you are not there. Maybe you hear your children complain about how little a babysitter plays with them and how much time the sitter spends on their phone, but your sitter denies it. A parent may decide the only way to alleviate their fears or confirm their suspicions is to have the ability to observe their babysitters throughout the day.

Once again this is a wisdom issue. And perhaps a better question to start with is: do I trust the individuals watching my children, or do I have any apprehension? If you have concern, you should stop and ask yourself why. Whether it is founded or unfounded, it is worth noticing and evaluating. You can then decide if you need to act upon your apprehensions. There is nothing more important than feeling as confident as possible that you have created a safe environment for your child when you are not present. If you ever question this, it is important to be willing to take a hard look at why and make some changes.

A camera will only serve to protect your children if you are up front and tell those who are in charge that they are being watched. If you choose to keep it a secret, you might catch a babysitter harming your child, but you will not be protecting your children from harm. Even with cameras, you are limited in what you can observe. You can see what is occurring in front of the camera. Once the babysitter is out of view, you have little clarity on what is unfolding.

If you choose to have cameras in your home, let your childcare providers know. It is forthright and it's a better way to secure the very thing you care most about: protecting your children from harm. It also sends the message that you are proactive and willing to check in on your children.

To be confident of the childcare provider you choose, be willing to ask many thoughtful (and at times uncomfortable) questions. By asking the right questions, you're bound to find the right applicant and avoid the wrong ones. Don't feel obligated to follow every suggestion included here. Some questions may be relevant for your family and some may not. Tailor these ideas to your home and family needs.

Here are some sample questions to ask a babysitter when checking in on them:

1. Tell me how the day went with the children. What went well? What did not? Notice, you are assuming they will have both good and potentially bad tidbits to fill you in on. This helps a babysitter who might be hesitant to tell you if your children were misbehaving.
2. What were you able to do with the kids while I was gone?
3. Did they spend any time outside? What did they do inside? How much time were they on technology?
4. Anything I need to know about how they ate or what they ate?
5. Anything else you think would be important for me to know?

Though this information seems obvious for a childcare provider to share, for a young or inexperienced babysitter, it may not be. By the time you get home, a childcare provider might be ready to rush out the door, or out to their next activity. Or a babysitter might be hesitant to share what they observed without an open invitation to do so. Good communication and expectations are essential to having a babysitter you can feel good about. It takes wisdom to decide what level of maturity and knowledge you expect from a childcare provider and when you are willing to do the work of training them. In any case, you are charged with the task of guarding your children against those who would harm them, as well as placing in their lives those who love and minister to them well. Using the guidelines and questions in this chapter will help you discern who is best suited to care for your child and also help you to evaluate how they are doing.

CHAPTER 13

Wisdom Issues: Safe Words and Family Safety Plans

"If any of you lacks wisdom, let him ask God, who gives generously to all without reproach, and it will be given him." James 1:5

Many parents incorporate safe words or passwords into their family's safety plan. For example, if a child is picked up unexpectedly by someone at school, an afterschool activity, or a friend's house, that individual would need to know what the safe word was so the child would know it was okay to leave with them. If someone showed up at your home while you were out, the individual would need to know the password before opening the door. If anyone they know wanted them to go with them and a child wasn't sure it was safe, a test could be whether that individual knows the safe word.

Safe words or phrases should be words that are not too commonly used but are not confusing to the family. It is helpful for the whole family to have a say in choosing the word, and it should be one that is easy to remember (but not easily guessed by strangers). Have it connected to something that makes sense to a child, like a fun word connected to an inside family joke or a favorite movie, or perhaps a made-up word or unique name.

As kids get older, it is also helpful to consider a safe word when they want to alert their parents or an adult that they need help getting out of a situation. A parent may send a child to a friend's house to play, but during the course of time, your daughter begins feeling uncomfortable around another child or adult who is demonstrating unsafe behavior. A phrase may be helpful when a child is with others and does not want to let on that they want help or would like to get away from someone. It might be something like, "Mom, I forgot to tell you that Uncle Charles called (knowing there is no Uncle Charles)."

Whatever the situation your child is experiencing—perhaps unwanted physical or sexual comments or behavior, aggressive or bullying behavior, or even a hostile home environment with an uncomfortable level of yelling and hostility in the home—it's important that your child has a way to safely reach out to you. If your child is using another parent's phone or feels afraid to say they are unsafe, it is helpful to have a code word or phrase they can speak that will alert you they need help. It could be a phrase life "Mom, remember when you told me to remind you to feed the hamster (the hamster you do not own)." Or "Dad, Bob said he will be late tonight." A phrase is often helpful because it cannot be detected as odd or out of the norm by someone standing close by listening. A parent can then say, "So you need my help?" or "Do you need me to come there right now?" A child can simply say yes or no. Then a parent decides to either get on the phone and find a reason to come get their child or they may choose to just show up unannounced and respond to whatever the situation requires.

Developing a Family Safety Plan

While we all hope and pray we will never need to use it, it is also important for your family to develop a safety plan for what to do if a variety of common potential emergencies arise, such as tornadoes, floods, fires, or even medical emergencies. It is a good idea to talk through what to do if any one of these scenarios arise.

Whether it is a fire escape plan, a tornado, a flood warning, a power outage, or intruder, knowing what to do and having a plan will help your family be less fearful and more prepared. Depending on where you live (city or rural, near water or cliffs), the type of natural disasters that are common to your area and the personal safety concerns your home might have will inform the type of safety plans that make sense for you to develop.

Some Practical Suggestions for Family Safety

- Fire or flood plan. If you live in an area prone to fires or floods, talk through how you'd want your family to respond in such an event, where to go if they need to flee the house, a meeting place if you got separated, how to get out of the home quickly, and what (if anything) to take with them. And, of course, house fires can happen anywhere so this is an important component of your family safety plan.
- Power outage. This may happen in storms or natural disasters. Do your children know where to find a flashlight they can access and know how to use it? How will they keep warm, find light sources, or preserve food? Some information will be unnecessary for children, but at other times it will make them feel more comfortable knowing the plan.
- Intruders and break-ins. Some kids are oblivious to such danger, but other kids may inherently fear intruders breaking into their homes. Use care in how you approach this topic so that you do not instill more fear in your child. Remember, we want to instill confidence and competence. Many kids never experience this, but talking about what to do will provide a measure of self-assurance. As uncomfortable as it might feel, discuss how to lock and check doors and windows, where to hide if they need to, and how long to stay quiet.
- Consider giving your children swimming lessons. Not only is it a good life skill and excellent exercise, it prevents kids from drowning or being fearful of water. Make sure kids learn water safety and know they aren't allowed in pools or large bodies of water unsupervised.

- Walk through your home and teach them about the potential hazards of each area. One of our kids once put a battery in his mouth and received quite a surprise. Once your child is old enough to understand, it's a quick thing to teach them about the dangers of fireplaces, electrocution, the stove, etc. Put up the appropriate child safety measures for young children as you educate older children.
- Older teens should learn what to do if the lights go out, when to avoid power sources, how to adjust heater or air conditioning units, and how to use the fireplace safely.
- When going away for an evening, overnight, or a weekend, have a plan for your children. Whether a sitter or an older sibling is left in charge, it is helpful to have all the kids know what to expect, how to help chip in, and who to reach out to for help.
- Write a fire escape plan together and let kids help brainstorm what to do and how to get out of the home. Have it laminated and posted inside a pantry or closet door where kids will have access to it; it is helpful to pull it out yearly, perhaps when changing smoke detector batteries. Review it with the whole family, make updates, or suggest changes.
- Have emergency numbers and contact information for people your kids may reach out to in an emergency. Write addresses, emails, phone numbers, who is available at what time, and who is the best to contact depending on the need.
- Practice the family code word. As mentioned earlier, it is a simple way to let your kids know someone is safe and they are trustworthy.
- Make sure you check smoke and carbon monoxide detectors, fire extinguishers, flashlight batteries, and emergency radios. Yearly or twice-yearly checks make sure they are still working.
- If a sibling has a medical condition, consider ways this might affect a family safety plan. Help your other children to

understand the need and how they can help. One of our children has a vision impairment. As a rule of thumb, we would always have a sibling partner with him or be an extra set of eyes for him when needed. As kids develop and become independent, the needs may vary. Siblings of children with food allergies can learn to spot an allergic reaction and need to know where to find an EpiPen® or other medications. Keep an emergency kit with medicine for various situations and medical reactions.

• Consider kids with special behavioral, emotional, and developmental needs in a family safety plan. Contemplate when it is and isn't helpful to talk through possible scenarios, how you would like a sibling to respond in a crisis or meltdown, who should be contacted, and what steps will be taken to account for a child's extra needs.

This is your family plan, so take the liberty to include anything you find helpful and delete what is unnecessary. Thoughtfulness, education, and wisdom will strengthen your family and make your children feel secure.

CHAPTER 14

How to Respond When Violence Touches Your Child's Life[16]

"Even though I walk through the valley of the shadow of death,
I will fear no evil,
for you are with me;
your rod and your staff,
they comfort me." Psalm 23:4

The threat of danger impacts our children on a regular basis. Tragic school shootings, violent crimes and the like all incite an array of heartache and anxiety. Even when the threat is not at our front door, it is booming from media outlets into our homes. The likelihood that your child is impacted in one way or another is high. Regardless of where you live or how stable your family life is, the lives of kids and teens are being touched by violence to some degree and we must help them make sense of it.

Engage with Your Kids Honestly but Not Fearfully

Rather than react out of fear, we must help our kids by demonstrating an appropriate level of sobriety and sorrow by such events, while exhibiting that our hope is in Christ. The challenge is to find the right balance—teaching young people awareness and caution, while equally encouraging trust in a sovereign God. The most hazardous thing we let our children do is to ride in a car, yet we rarely fear driving them to school or church, or the mall—nor should we. Young people must learn to live life fully, and not be overshadowed by fear.

So parents—engage with your kids about these threatening realities. Do your best to explain them and be willing to discuss why evil exists. Model godly grief and educate your children on what is right and just. Our kids will be able to walk with confidence in a troubled world if they are educated on how to think, feel equipped to respond, and have grown to put their confidence in their Creator. We want to teach children how to both navigate this world, and trust an unrivaled God.

Five Suggestions to Help Children Feel Prepared in the Face of Potential Violence

1. Have a plan for potential dangers. We know it is helpful to have a fire escape plan at home, school, and work. Likewise, help kids develop a plan they can follow when they become aware of possible violence. Being prepared does not avoid the event, but gives a child a sense of confidence that he or she can respond well and get through it safely.

2. Role-play, role-play, role-play. As you instruct your children on what they should do in various types of emergencies, do so in a calm and matter-of-fact manner, being sure not to frighten them by talking about it. Then, practice. Describe hypothetical situations and have them tell you what they would say or do. This helps children to react efficiently and swiftly in a high pressure situation.

3. Be a safe, trusting adult to go to and identify other safe adults that can help in a crisis. If your kids know in advance who to go to for help in an emergency, they will feel less fear. To the extent possible, be sure these people (including yourself!) are able to offer appropriate comfort, poise, and direction based on the situation. This means being able to respond in a way that

neither minimizes nor overreacts to the threat at hand. A balanced response during and after an emergency will help your children going forward.

4. Lead them to the God of all comfort. "Do not be afraid" is mentioned 365 times in the Bible. The solution to fearful situations is always God's presence. He offers himself as our comfort, strength and portion. Look for ways to make this tangible and real in a young person's life. Perhaps you can memorize with them Psalm 23 and then remind them that Jesus is their good shepherd and will be with them even in the darkest valley.

5. Know what Scripture has to say about life, tribulations, and sufferings. When kids ask why something terrible happened, it is important to give simple and honest answers. Young people need to make sense out of life accurately and redemptively. Help them look beyond present sufferings and remind them a faithful God cares for them. God's will for their life cannot be thwarted. As Jeremiah 29:11 states, "For I know the plans I have for you, declares the Lord, plans for welfare and not for evil, to give you a future and a hope."

We cannot promise young people that tragic events will not happen, but we can give them the knowledge and resources to navigate such events. The better equipped they feel, the less anxious they will be. Equally important is the reality that kids will always be making sense out of their experiences. The question is, will they do so accurately? It is imperative that our kids grow up with a worldview that is biblical (accurately interprets the world we live in) redemptive (God takes what is broken and restores/make all things new) and hope-filled (confidence in the character of God and anticipation for the good he will do). We can all pray that violence will not directly touch our children's lives, but in the meantime, wisdom prepares them in case it does.

Part Three

EQUIPPING TEENAGERS AND YOUNG ADULTS WITH SAFETY SKILLS

CHAPTER 15

Teenagers Need Genuine Relationships with God and Their Parents

"The fear of the LORD is the beginning of knowledge; fools despise wisdom and instruction." (Proverbs 1:7)

Perhaps the greatest safety skill we can offer our young people is the willingness to pursue truth. This is the starting point of wisdom because it points them to a relationship with the God who made them and loves them. We live in an age where young people believe they are entitled to live life their way, follow their own truth, and create and recreate their identity. Our teenagers need to see that there is a loving, sovereign God who is the author of their story and the one who defines truth and error, good and evil. He is writing the script of their lives, and it is a far better story than they can write for themselves. He's sovereign, faithful, kind, and is worthy of our trust and allegiance. We need to woo our teens to their loving heavenly Father, instead of reducing church and Christianity to a list of moral dos and don'ts. Our children need a real relationship with someone who has entered into their experiences and has something to say to them. They need to know that God loves them and establishes his ways to help them thrive.

Ephesians 5:15–16 says, "Be very careful, then, how you live—not as unwise but as wise, making the most of every opportunity, because the days are evil" (NIV) In a developmental stage where all common sense seems to go out the window, it is crucial for us to help our teens develop the muscles of wisdom and discernment to navigate the many trials they will be facing.

Too often when teaching safety skills, we come up with rules and formulas for trying to protect our kids from every evil. Instead of approaching our teenagers and young adult children this way, we should be encouraging them to adopt the biblical principles related to discernment, wisdom, and relationships. These principles are founded on their relationship with the living God—it's their heavenly Father who will guide them through any difficulty that might arise. Learning biblical principles becomes the backdrop for how young people figure out life, evaluate behavior, recognize poor character, detect deceit and danger, and pursue mature friends and mentors. The more we instill these things in our children, the more they will become second nature and the more equipped they will be to live wisely as they become independent.

Teens Need Relationships with Their Parents

For many parents, the teenage years can be both liberating as their teens become more independent and simultaneously a source of anxiety as teens are also navigating new trials and temptations. Although many parents approach the teen years with trepidation, these years can be an unprecedented opportunity for teens to grow in their relationship with God and with their parents. You might think teens need you less as they grow older, but, make no mistake about it, they need you just as much, but in different ways than when they were younger.

God places loving authority in the hands of parents. It is our responsibility to lead, oversee, and direct our homes in a wise, prayerful, and godly manner. Loving, gracious authority is trustworthy, judicious, and benevolent and it also understands the need to direct, instruct, and establish rules. It models Christlike influence and points children to a God they can trust and follow.

But teens often rebel, rejecting parental authority. Sometimes this is due to defiance within the young person. Other times, it may be due to the influence of their peers or may reflect the strong aversion to authority found in our culture. When teens respond in rebellion or defiance, we often attempt to reinstate our parental rights by quoting Scripture and demanding that children comply. But most teenagers do not bow their heads and humbly repent of their ways when parents do this. Rather, they respond with a readiness to battle for control and independence.

I believe the responsibility for much of this lies with us parents. Often, in the way we structure our lives, we repeatedly, though usually unknowingly, give up our parenting role and give it over to others. Much of our time is spent occupying our children and reacting to them, rather than engaging them in relationship. Our kids are in school all day and then are often involved in sports, music lessons, gymnastics, or even church activities. When kids are home, they are doing homework, are occupied by their phones, or are gaming. In short, we have become irrelevant to much of their daily experience. Given our absence from so much of their lives—and the increase of peer and cultural influence—why would our kids continue to accept our authority?

Activities and busy schedules limit our opportunities to influence our kids. Active lifestyles are not wrong, yet we must be aware of how much time we are engaging our kids in meaningful relationship versus keeping them happily occupied. One fosters intimacy, the other fosters passive detachment. Do not be mistaken—kids do look for guidance and authority, and when they need it, they will likely turn to the influence that has captured their admiration and trust; this is often their peer group.

Building Relationship and Influence as Children Grow

Parental powerlessness is difficult to face. Sometimes we minimize and excuse it, but we cannot just accept it as inevitable or chalk it up to "teenage attitudes" or "kids these days." Though our role and influence change as our children grow, we still need to be a voice in their lives. But regaining that impact does not come about through coercion, bribery, or threats. It comes through relationship and time spent together.

To holistically fulfill our parental responsibilities, we need to prioritize building relationships with our teens that display care, sacrificial giving, genuine compassion, and being there for them. The more gracious and godly authority we exhibit, the more our children will desire to follow and submit to it.

A strong, godly relationship serves our teenage and young adult children in many ways. Here are a few:

- It creates an atmosphere of respect, admiration, and cooperation.
- It evokes security and connection with children.
- It fosters a healthy dependence upon parents for spiritual and emotional nurturing.
- It models dependency on wise counsel outside ourselves and ultimately on the Lord.
- It models a properly ordered respect for leadership and governance.
- It builds trust when we encourage certain responses or discourage particular choices.

Fostering these qualities in our kids imparts an integrity to daily life and prepares them to thrive in the world they will live in. When we have established trust and influence in our teenagers' lives, we can feel more confident that if and when they face dangerous or concerning situations, we will have a voice.

Parental authority is not about force, power, or dominance. It is about trust and wise influence. It is about relationship and Christlike leadership that values the good and safety of those being led. Instead of becoming more authoritarian with your kids, invest in your relationship with them. Show them you care and are committed to their good. It may not be well received at first, and it may take time. You may need to limit their number of extracurricular activities, time with their peers, and the multitude of ways your family gets pulled away from each other, but the results are well worth the effort. A loving parent/teen relationship is one the greatest safety skills you can give them. And it will model for them the love of their heavenly Father.

If you don't know where to start, simply begin asking questions about their life and their world. Find out what they enjoy doing, what activities or past times they are drawn to, and why. Ask good open-ended questions (so they can't answer with a simple "yes" or "no"). Ask them to share about their day, or their opinion about things that are inconsequential (the latest movie that came out or the pizza you ordered for dinner) and things that are consequential (the legalization of marijuana or a peer who is making poor choices). Every attempt on your part, whether they are initially responsive or not, demonstrates your desire to know them.

It may feel wearisome and seem to bear little fruit, but press on and "let us not grow weary of doing good, for in due season we will reap, if we do not give up" (Galatians 6:9).

CHAPTER 16

Comparison, Peer Pressure, and Treating Others with Respect

"The fear of man lays a snare,
but whoever trusts in the LORD is safe." Proverbs 29:25

The Bible identifies "fear of man" as a core human struggle—all of us struggle with caring more about what people think of us than we should. We all will struggle with the temptation to please the people in our lives instead of living for God's approval. For teens, the desire for acceptance and to define who they are and where they belong in the world makes them particularly susceptible to living for the approval of their peer group. But doing so is dangerous. We have all noticed what the apostle Paul said, that "Bad company ruins good morals (1 Corinthians 15:33)." Teenagers will be tempted to compare themselves with their peers and to try to conform to those norms. They will be vulnerable to feelings of inadequacy, discontent, or envy when they see the values, norms, and friend groups around them and feel they can't quite hit the mark.

How does comparison threaten your teen? One of our kids is drawn to sports figures, the latest sneakers and what all his baseball pals are wearing. Another child is drawn to talk and act like his drama friends. Still another wants to be online gaming and have the newest electronic devices. Pinterest, Facebook, and Instagram tempt our other teen. She watches how her peers are dressing and conforms her attire to the latest trends.

The Pitfalls of Comparison

To varying degrees, we are always evaluating other people's behaviors and choices and comparing them to our own. The danger lies in the weight your child gives to these evaluations. Does it become their standard for measuring significance and meaningfulness? Does their life's value increase or decrease based on how they think they measure up? John 12:43 says, "They loved the glory that comes from man more than the glory that comes from God." It is the struggle of every child who wants to fit in with their peers. Are they living for the praise of their peers or to please God?

Comparison breeds lies and leads to temptation and unwise conformity. It produces:

- Jealousy and envy: What they have is "better." They grow to believe that good things are given to others, but not to them. It tempts teens to covet or strive after attaining what another has.
- Discontentment: What I have is "less than." Whether it's wealth, social status, or relationships, if they don't have what those around them seem to have, they begin to believe God is withholding good from them.
- Inadequacy: Who I am is "less than." Teens can easily believe they will never measure up. They feel inadequate in relationships, friendships, or life circumstances. Insecurity takes root.
- Lack of authenticity: They struggle to be vulnerable or transparent so no one will see their flaws. Struggles, weakness, and brokenness are seen as defects needing to be concealed.
- Short-sightedness: Teens forget the treasure that is waiting for them in eternity and live only for the moment. They must be given a vision for the future that is far better, far more worth yearning for.

When teens fall into comparison, they shift their desire to live for what is right and good and forget their ultimate purpose is to know and love God and to make him known. Others either become a threat to them or a measuring stick to gauge their worth. This will take them down the path of adapting and conforming to the world around them.

We can help them live with differences, strengths and weaknesses, blessings and struggles, successes and failures, because we struggle with the exact same temptations. As we turn to God, he helps us. As we encourage them to turn to God, he will also help them to stand in the midst of their peers with self-assurance and individuality. The more they are able to do so, the less they will be prone to giving into peer pressure and making unwise decisions.

Imagine the teenage boy who knows the right thing to do, but like most, doesn't want to stand out as different. So, when crude joking happens, he laughs and hides that it bothers him. A week later, the same friends are all on an app where they send memes and message each other. He decides to go on his phone and download the app so he can fit in with his friends. As time goes on, he joins in on the inappropriate comments, cursing, and when a young girl offers to send nude photos, he accepts. It can be a slippery slope of one bad decision opening the door for many more poor choices to follow.

Perhaps your daughter lives on social media and sees her friends buying the latest trends and makeup and snapping photos of themselves. They are now creating their own channel and growing in popularity. Your daughter is desperately wanting to fit in and be admired too. She secretly resents her friends and begins to seek ways to outdo them. She begins to make derogatory comments online and tries to create a rumor to discredit the girls in her peer group.

You cannot compliment someone you are competing against. They become a rival, rather than a friend or fellow struggler. Your teen shifts from being a person who cares for those around them, to one who must keep up with or become better than their peers.

Rather than competing against each other, we want to raise teens who come alongside and build each other up. Like Jesus, we want to encourage our teens to seek to serve more than to be served and to feel secure in who they are in the Lord so they can stand confidently.

Tips for Fighting Peer Pressure and Comparison

How do we teach our kids to fight peer pressure and comparison? Here are four ways:

1. Identify with them how challenging it is to be occupied and distracted by the world's value system. Our desires, discontentment, jealousy, and inadequacy grow when we try to get our sense of worth and approval from anything outside of our relationship with the Lord. Christ offers to free us all from the burden of living by the praise of our peers. Tell them how he has helped you with this struggle. (John 12:43; Colossians 3:23)
2. Deflect the comparison others might place upon them. There will be people who try to make them feel less than enough. Teach them that they have a choice about whether or not they allow peer pressure to shape them. (Isaiah 2:22; Matthew 10:28)
3. Teach them to live before the face of God, not before others on social media. We need to woo our kids to God's ways. The more you make it look good to them, the more they will want to reflect God's character and his ways in their life. Help them fix their eyes on what is unseen, not what is seen. (2 Corinthians 5:9; Colossians 1:9–10)

Instead of living as rivals in this world, we can teach our kids to live with their peers as iron sharpening iron; desiring to bring out Christlikeness in one another. Comparison dulls each of us; Christlikeness sharpens, refines, and equips our kids to stand against peer pressure.

As we daily instill this in our teens, they will be free to evaluate choices, lifestyles, and the behavior of others in a way that will help them grow (not define them or give them worth). Godly evaluation gives room for differences that complement and sharpen one another, not rank each other's value. When their value is rooted in our Creator, kids are free to appreciate one another's differences and individuality.

This establishes the foundation for all that is to follow. If we model and work to instill character, dignity, and distinctly biblical convictions, our young people will still face temptations, struggles, peer pressure, and other hazards, but they will be safeguarded against such things by their love for God and their love for people. They will have the tools and knowledge they need to "discern what is pleasing to the Lord" (Ephesians 5:10).

Language and Respect

> But sexual immorality and all impurity or covetousness must not even be named among you, as is proper among saints. Let there be no filthiness nor foolish talk nor crude joking, which are out of place, but instead let there be thanksgiving. (Ephesians 5:3–4)

You may wonder what language has to do with safety. Speech is an indicator of many internal realities. First, what comes out of the mouth is reflective of what is going on in the heart. We know that "out of the abundance of the heart [the] mouth speaks" (Luke 6:45). Teaching our kids to guard their hearts is the first line of defense to protect them from going down all kinds of destructive paths, ones that can cause harm to others or paths that open them up to harm. Teach young people that how they talk and how others talk matters. It is a window into a person's inner world, their thinking and worldview, and it is another way to evaluate character, actions, beliefs, and values.

Second, the way we speak demonstrates respect or disrespect. It either values or degrades the dignity of another. Teens can especially be known for mocking and crude joking with one another. It is often done in the name of fun but it has a cutting nature toward others. It creates fun at the expense of another, or at the expense of what is good, right, and pure. It is the opposite of letting speech be seasoned with grace, that it may give life to all who hear (Colossians 4:6).

Third, speech is an indicator of potential behavior. Crude or demeaning speech toward another is a step toward objectification and potential violence or mistreatment. We particularly tend to see this in the way young men speak about women and girls. The more your son speaks of women in ways that are objectifying, the more likely he is to treat a woman in an objectifying way. Girls can speak in ways that are objectifying as well, though statistically more males will mistreat females as a result of crude speech.

A teen who is taught to be respectful will be easily recognized by the way they talk to others. It is often reflective of an individual with personal conviction and character. When a teenager has character, conviction, and deeply held personal values, they are more discerning of those who are not.

Teens and their friends can certainly hide poor behavior behind respectful words, but that too will come out when their actions belie their words. Proverbs tells us, "As in water face reflects face, so the heart of man reflects the man" (Proverbs 27:19). We all know people who speak well in front of those they wish to deceive or impress, then reveal their real character when an adult or parent leaves the room. When you have raised young people to discern this, they will quickly see through it and be on guard. They will recognize good influences from those that are corrupt.

When God asked Samuel to anoint a new king, instead of Saul, he encouraged Samuel not to evaluate a person the way the world does: "Do not look on his appearance or on the height of his stature, because I have rejected him. For the LORD sees not as man sees: man looks at the outward appearance, but the LORD looks on the heart" (1 Samuel 16:7). Our children often fall into the trap of looking at the appearances of those around them, for what is good and right, or even "normal." When our children do so, they lose sight of God and his ways. Our job is to woo them to God's ways, and demonstrate the rich life it provides for "where your treasure is, there your heart will be also" (Matthew 6:21).

CHAPTER 17

Sex and Dating

"Look carefully then how you walk, not as unwise but as wise, making the best use of the time, because the days are evil. Therefore do not be foolish, but understand what the will of the Lord is."
Ephesians 5:15–17

How do you talk to your teens about sex and sexuality? It can be an uncomfortable subject. But the more you and I are willing to get over our own discomfort with this subject, the better we will be able to help shape our children's understanding of this subject from a biblical worldview and help them be aware of a variety of personal safety concerns. Also, as mentioned previously, it is important for our kids to be intentionally taught to think about and speak to the opposite sex in respectful ways.

Hopefully you have been speaking about these matters well before your kids become teenagers. As I said earlier in the book, it is far better to proactively shape our children's view on sex than to go back and try to debunk something they have heard from peers or media. If you have waited to discuss sex until a child becomes a teenager, you've already left them to their own, or the surrounding culture's, perspective to try to figure life out.

God Creates, the World Corrupts
Here is a phrase I often use when we talk to our kids about sex: God creates; the world corrupts. God creates food; the world corrupts the

use of food. God creates relationships; the world corrupts and uses relationships in ways that were never intended. God creates sex and sexuality; the world corrupts sex and turns it into something it was never meant to be.

Although this is true, too often we address the corruption of such things *before* building a positive perspective of what God created them to be. By the time we engage youth on a topic like sex, it is often packed full of warnings—what you shouldn't do and why you shouldn't do it. Sadly, what comes across is that God is against sex because it is immoral or unhealthy, and a young person might draw the conclusion that it is sinful and wrong to have sexual desires.

Actually, God is not against sex—he is all for it. After all, he is the author of sex, and all that God creates is good. In a pleasure-saturated society, we can offer a distinct message about sex that is more compelling than the recklessness of the world. As Christians we should be sharing with our children a positive, celebratory view of a protected gift. We need to be willing to convey this message to our young people sooner and do so in a way that is clear, positive, and bold.

We need to help our teens understand that when we start with a corrupt view of sex and use it in ways God did not intend, it will not deliver the lasting joy and intimacy that God intended for sex to have in a faithful marriage.

Everything that it is created is meant to function well within a specific context. Sometimes I use the example of the iPhone to illustrate this truth. The iPhone is an amazing piece of technology that can do more things than I can name. But imagine dropping the phone off a highway bridge, only to be surprised that when you retrieve it from the pavement below it no longer works. Then imagine blaming Apple for your phone's shattered state and filing a complaint that you have been given defective equipment! Do you see how foolish it would be to blame the creator when, clearly, you were provided the boundaries in which the phone was to work and it was you who chose to misuse it?

The creator of something knows how it is intended to work best. Any time you go outside of the creator's parameters, it will malfunction. God is not a killjoy. He created sex and set the context in which it is meant to thrive: in the marriage relationship between one man and one woman. We must inspire our kids to have confidence that the context in which God calls us to enjoy sex is for our good. He wants to keep us safe, and wants sex to thrive in a safe, committed, loving relationship—as he defines it.

When I talk with my young counselees about sex and God's plan and design, I hope to surprise them with some positive truths. Many will never have heard them before. We talk together about how God created sex, it is good and right, and you should want it in the right context.

Subsequently, we will also talk about what happens when you corrupt sex and use it in ways that God never intended. Though the world tells us that you should be free to do whatever feels right to you, whenever and with whomever you please, this approach to sex will not deliver what it promises. Instead, it will deliver painful consequences: emotional brokenness, shattered dreams, relational injury, potential health consequences from sexually transmitted diseases, and unplanned pregnancies. Sex used like this becomes warped and unrecognizable, a degraded picture of what it was created to be. It may deliver temporary pleasure, but it cannot provide lasting satisfaction and relational harmony.

Principles to Guide Your Conversations

If you struggle to know how to engage your kids on potentially uncomfortable topics such as this, consider the following principles to help shape your approach.

First, talk in positive ways. Model an affirming, godly view of sexuality. When we talk to our kids about sex, we try to speak in a positive, affirming manner. If not from you, where will they hear it? We have even set a challenge as a family for each of us to find two or three passages where the Bible speaks of sex in positive ways. We have gone over together Genesis 2:25, Song of Solomon, Proverbs 5:18–19, among others. Imagine the look on your teenager's face when you challenge them to do this! It is essential they see the beauty of sex as God created it, not simply all the ways it has been corrupted. Sexuality is good and enjoyable when rightly ordered in our lives. It is part of who we are and how we live out our lives before the Lord.

Second, talk often. Talking to kids about sex (or any important subject) should never be a one-time conversation. Children and teens are always processing, thinking, and coming up with new questions, and trying to make sense of it all. They will be hit with new issues at each stage of development. Make sure they are not processing these challenges and questions alone. Actively pursue conversations with them.

Third, talk freely. Foster a spirit of openness in your home and in your relationship with your children. Let them know that no topic is off limits, too hard, or too embarrassing to talk about. The more comfortable you are in talking freely, the more likely you are to make your kids comfortable and listen to what you have to say about sexuality.

Encourage questions and conversation whenever you can. For example, when you are in the car together, find reasons to ask what their friends are talking about at school or how their teachers are discussing sexuality. Ask your kids what they think about what they are hearing. After a movie, ask them questions about the attitudes or lifestyles you just saw portrayed on the screen. Give them freedom to have opinions and voice them; it is a window into their thoughts. You will then know how to pray and better speak into their lives.

Fourth, talk soon. We live in a culture that promotes a self-absorbed, sensuality-centered lifestyle. If our children are going to learn about sexuality at earlier and earlier ages (and they will), be the one to proactively shape a godly vision of sex. We live in a sex-crazed culture that threatens to form your child's morality. You cannot afford to remain silent. We want our kids to grow up knowing how God intended life, relationships, and sexuality to be lived out. Young people will hear the voice that is the loudest or the most persuasive. Let it be God's voice in and through you.

Some examples of topics to talk through:

- God's design for gender and sexuality
- A biblical view of marriage
- What it means to live faithfully as sexual beings
- What it looks like to pursue someone you are interested in
- How to conduct yourself in a romantic relationship
- What is appropriate physical affection in romantic relationships and what is not

Dating and Relationships

When you teach young people to show respect for others, it transfers over to showing respect for the opposite sex. What does it look like for a young man to show respect for a girl who is a friend? What about a girl he is interested in dating? Likewise, what does it look like for a girl to show that same respect for a guy she is friends with or hopes to date?

Mutual respect is vitally important for mothers and fathers to model for their children because their peer group will model something vastly different. The way fifteen-year-old boys typically speak about the opposite sex will be radically different from the way you want your daughter spoken about or spoken to. Your sons need to know what it looks and sounds like to honor all of the women in their lives, whether it be their mother, sister, classmate, or a girl they'd like to date. Likewise, the way your daughters are raised will inform how they speak to and about their fathers, brothers, classmates, or a young man they are interested in.

You want your children to be able to engage well socially and relationally. The more you model this and give them opportunity to practice, the more comfortable, the more confident and more competent they will be in engaging well in most social situations.

Families may have different ideas on what dating should or shouldn't look like or at what age it is appropriate, but I think we can all agree that the healthiest relationships will form when young people learn how to engage respectfully, wisely, and genuinely with one another. Having this modeled in the home is one of the best ways to do this. Talk openly with your young people about your expectations and views for dating and engaging with their peers.

Your rules about dating (age, context, etc.) are wisdom issues for each home. Wherever you land, it is important to have principles that undergird the decisions you make and principles that help your children make good decisions. You must discern whether you'd like them to date in groups, encourage them to do things in public, or have guidelines about spending too much time alone or in private places. Having good conversations about spending too much time together, and the need to foster good friendships outside of a dating relationship are ways of broadening their world and ideas about what a romantic relationship should look like. Remember, they are receiving messages all day from their peers, dating relationships they observe, and media telling them what makes for a good relationship. Proactively inform their views and help them foster healthy ideas about love, romance, and dating.

For example, many parents set rules about the age a son or daughter must be in order to date, but they don't consider the maturity or character of their child (or the person he or she is interested in). What good is a rule about the age of dating if your son or daughter lacks the discernment or character to pursue a healthy relationship?

Parents should focus more of their time fostering conversations and ideas about what to look for in a dating relationship than on the rules that will go with dating—although they are important. It is also important to help a teen know who they are and who God wired them to be so that they are not allowing others to change them in an effort to feel accepted or loved by someone they are interested in romantically.

Consent

Consent is a popular term being used today to help both younger and older kids understand the need to respect other people's comfort level, particularly regarding physical contact or signs of affection. Consent often refers to never pressuring another person to do something physically or sexually that they're uncomfortable doing. With younger children, we teach them that when someone hugs them, pats them, or touches them in any way that makes them uncomfortable, they need to be able to tell you so you can be aware of the situation and help evaluate what's going on or why they are uncomfortable. As kids get older, it is important to teach them to ask permission to show someone affection, listening when they say no, and learning how to ask someone to stop.

This concept is particularly important in dating relationships in the teen years. Talking about consent means talking about the biblical values behind respect for other people. We want our kids to always act with integrity and personal conviction based on God's standards. We want them to show respect, honor, and kindness to others. It is important to talk through what this looks like in a dating relationship or a dating context. Talk to your teenager about what type of affection is appropriate and why. Have conversations about how they should respond and can respond if somebody pressures them physically or sexually.

Brainstorm possible scenarios and encourage them to talk about ways they see this unfolding at school or in their peer group. Your teenager may be hesitant to express what they're thinking or feeling, but they're often quite open to share what the kids in their school are saying and doing. Ask, "What are kids in your class doing when it comes to dating?" This gives you a window into what is being modeled to them as well as how they might be tempted. A good follow up question is often, "Tell me what you think about that situation? How would you respond if it were you?"

Principles for Preparing Your Children to Date

Once again, teach them to evaluate character. Does this person share the same faith and values? How do they demonstrate it? What is their behavior like? How do they treat other friends or the opposite sex? How do they treat their parents and siblings? Do they have good relationships with their family or poor ones? And why? Are they involved in extracurricular activities, hobbies, or church events? What are their future goals or dreams? What are the person's strengths and weaknesses? How do you think that might impact you if you are dating them and in a relationship?

Questions to Consider before Dating

Get your teen to analyze their own mindset about dating. What is their reason for wanting to date in the first place? What qualities are they looking for in a boyfriend/girlfriend and potential future spouse? What nonnegotiable traits must a potential girlfriend or boyfriend have, and what are the negotiable ones? Nonnegotiable traits may be: Do they get along with people, respect authority, go to church, share similar values? Negotiable characteristics could be things such as humor level, educational background, and shared hobbies and experiences.

More specifics may develop as your teen gets older, but it's helpful for them to understand that who they date will influence who they eventually marry. Do they want to eventually marry someone who is trustworthy, kind, and seeks to know and honor the Lord? Then that is who they should date. It is valuable to discuss the reasons behind their voiced negotiable and nonnegotiable traits.

Evaluating Their Own Strengths and Weaknesses

Another important way to coach your teenager when it comes to dating is to talk about their own strengths and weaknesses. Do they follow through with their commitments? Do they easily lose their temper? Is there a pattern of excessive laziness in their lives? While teens should never feel pressured to change their personality or the essence of themselves in order to attract someone, this can be a helpful opportunity to do some healthy self-examination to see if they are developing the same type of character traits they would want to find in someone they date. At the same time, encourage them to be comfortable with who they are so they are not trying to change for the person they are with, and help them see the importance of dating somebody who is willing to accept them for who they are.

Dating and Levels of Maturity

Discuss with your teen how you view dating at their age and level of development. Do you encourage them to remain friends and get to know a variety of different people, learning to relate to them and discover what you enjoy about different peers? Do you encourage exclusive relationships at their age and why? Parents vary greatly in their views on this. Make sure you have solid reasons to give your son or daughter when you share your view. Help them see how it benefits them, and what you hope they will learn. When it comes to the early years of dating, you may want to encourage your teens not to jump immediately into serious relationships but to instead spend time getting to know various people on a friendship level. This can help them evaluate the type of person they want to pursue. Do you believe your teen should only go out on group dates and not one-on-one? There are many different views about these things, and it's a wisdom call to decide what is most beneficial for your child and why.

Good Practices for Dating

Talk to your teen about good practices when he or she is on a date. They need to learn how to practice things like chivalry, good conversation, how to meet somebody's parents, what type of questions to ask to get to know somebody, how to discern a person's beliefs, etc. Help them think through what is respectful, enjoyable, and beneficial for both parties on a date. Discuss whether it is appropriate to ask somebody out through text, in person, or on the phone, and why.

Fostering these types of conversations and principles in your children is far better than simply establishing rules about when they can date and who they can date. Instead, you are teaching your children to wisely discern and evaluate the type of relationships they should pursue and why they are drawn to certain people. We always want our children to grow in wisdom and discernment, and we know the people they pursue or are pursued by have tremendous influence over them. The more equipped your teenagers are to evaluate who they want to date, the more they will be protected from the risk of settling for the first person who shows an interest in them. The more you teach them what wise, healthy relationships look like, the more you give them discernment to steer clear of unwise, unhealthy ones.

Your child's peer group will always be trying to influence this decision and will try to hook them up with friends and peers that may or may not be good for them. Their peers will buck against your rules and ideas, but if you have spent years preparing your kids and instilling these beliefs in them and they have accepted them as their own, they are more likely to stand on their principles and be spared from a world of hazards.

Practical Safety Tips for Dating

Even before your teen starts to date, you can also discuss with them some important safety tips when it comes to dating. Some of these guidelines won't apply as much when they are younger and are more likely to hang out with friends in groups or are in more closely supervised settings, but either way, these are important topics to cover with them so they can be prepared for an array of possible scenarios that could compromise their safety.

- Know where your teenager is going and check in with them. Talk through what makes for a good curfew and why it is wise to have one.
- Always ask to meet your teenager's date and take the time to get to know them.
- Have a conversation about ways your teenager can get out of a dating situation that makes them uncomfortable. Tell them they can always use you as an excuse and tell their date a parent requires them at home. Additionally, give them permission to say no if they are uncomfortable with a situation.

Make sure you talk through with them what is uncomfortable and ways to handle awkward moments.

- Talk about meeting in public places and choosing activities that foster conversation and interaction.
- Make them aware of the need to keep track of their own food and drink. Leaving food and drinks unattended can provide an opportunity for them to be tampered with or drugged.
- Encourage them to respond if something makes them uncomfortable. The more you build confidence and discernment in your teens, the more likely they are to respond in the moment when something feels uncomfortable or inappropriate.
- Talk to your kids about the hard issues, such as: dating abuse, date rape, belittling, sexting, sexual pressure, and the issues of consent and what that means to you.
- Consider discouraging your teenagers from online dating. Online dating is not morally wrong and can have some benefits, but as teenagers, there are far too many pitfalls that are difficult to navigate at their age (see next section).

There are so many topics and discussions a parent can and should have on this topic—and they must be ongoing discussions with your kids. When you do not know how to broach a certain topic with your teen, turn to trusted resources. There are good books, podcasts, blogs, sermons and age-appropriate materials you can turn to. No one resource can cover everything exhaustively, but you can find many options for bringing up hard topics and talking about them with your kids. Consider asking other parents who have recently navigated these issues what they did and how they came to the decisions that they did. Ask them what resources were helpful to them. We want our kids to grow in the skill of living wisely, discerning God's will, and being faithful in their conduct. It takes thought, wisdom, and care to know how to navigate these issues, be willing to do the hard work of helping your teens think wisely about dating.

CHAPTER 18

Social Media and Technology Safety

"Trust in the Lord with all your heart, and do not lean on your own understanding. In all your ways, acknowledge him, and he will make straight your paths. Be not wise in your own eyes; fear the Lord, and turn away from evil." Proverbs 3:5–7

One of the many hard things about the teen years is that most teenagers are "wise in their own eyes." They believe they know what is best for their life and that things are not as bad or wrong as their parents might believe. So, they avoid turning from evil and foolishly enter in, often completely unaware of the consequence that may follow.

Ryan was a thirteen-year-old boy who was caught cheating on a school assignment. When he got home, his parents were waiting for him, armed with a lecture and consequences to enforce. Angry and upset, Ryan stormed to his room, went to his social media account, and blurted out a post that read, "I hate my life—I just want to die." Thirty minutes later, Ryan was working on homework when there was a knock on the front door. His mother was greeted by two police officers and an ambulance. They were responding to a crisis call made by the parent of one of Ryan's peers who saw the post online and had understandably expressed concern for Ryan.

In a moment of anger and impulse, Ryan had vented his feelings publicly, oblivious of the repercussions of his actions. A moment of irrational emotion turned into hours and days of crisis intervention, suicide assessment, and mandated counseling.

Risks and Repercussions of Social Media

I know many families who have had a similar experience with police showing up at their door, responding to posts made on social media by teens. Sometimes the posts are angry, full of threatening words toward another person, and other times they are a cry of despair that looks like (and may be) an attempt at suicide. Moments of teenage angst, frustration, and despair are not new. However, the ability to announce it on a public forum and to spread like wildfire is a new phenomenon. Momentary excessive reactions can cause long-term unnecessary consequences that are hard to undo.

The ability to vent unfiltered thoughts and feelings behind the safety of a screen, the perceived privacy of looking up pornography or sending and receiving naked photos, the ability to create and recreate your online persona, and the willingness to say or do things you would never consider doing to anyone's face opens wide the door of risk and serious repercussions to young people.

Social media also impacts the emotional stability of young people. In a 2021 advisory by Admiral Vivek Murthy, he reports a disturbing trend. Evidence shows an "alarming increase" in teen mental health problems, with one in three high school students and half of female students reporting persistent feelings of hopelessness or sadness.[17] Social media is indicated to be a primary contributor, with, 81% of fourteen- to twenty-two-year-olds reporting they used social media either "daily" or "almost constantly."[18] Living in the highly curated, artificial reality of Instagram, TikTok, Snapchat, and other social media platforms exposes young people to an enormous list of risks: body shame and eating disorders, social isolation, bullying, exposure to sexually explicit content and grooming by pedophiles, and more.

This study is not an anomaly. If you search online for the topic of kids and social media, you will find a plethora of reports from The Center for Disease and Control, the Atlantic Monthly, the National

Library of Medicine, Common Sense Media, and many other organizations detailing the negative impact of social media and constant technology use on children and teens.

What is the lesson for parents? If a mountain of research demonstrates concern for our children, are we as parents taking heed? Are we buying into the belief that children acquiring personal electronic devices and social media is an automatic rite of passage? Do we fear being accused of being the "only parent" who doesn't allow their preteen to have a phone, who uses parental controls, or who requires an open-device policy? Do we allow what other parents and other families are doing to inform what we choose to accept as normal? We must consider carefully how to make wise decisions about what we allow our children access to. We must be willing to stand in the gap and make some hard decisions about the best way to guard our children's hearts and minds; they can so easily be harmed or corrupted by the things of this world.

Establishing Guidelines, Expectations, and Oversight of Social Media and Other Technology

Regardless of when and how your kids end up using technology, talk to your kids about what to expect with social media use and why. Tell them you know things like sexting, cyberbullying, and the like happen to teens, and if they ever feel it is happening to them, you want to know *and will support them.* Over and over, kids need to hear that their parents will not be angry or punitive if they've made some missteps online but will come alongside their kids and support them as they figure out how to disentangle themselves from hard things that are happening.

If you do choose to allow your kids to be online, do your research and set up good parameters for your kids. Here are some ways you can consider setting up healthy guardrails for your child's online presence:

- Establish early on the principles of stewardship and accountability. You want your family to learn to steward all areas of life well. All they have been given is both a privilege and responsibility, including technology. With such responsibility, comes accountability and the willingness to be transparent and answerable for how they manage what they are given.

- As mentioned earlier, always have parental controls for family devices. Regardless of the standards you establish for your home, it is important to have boundaries and safety nets for your kids. Parental controls give families the ability to filter out graphic and unwanted content. It allows you to manage the amount of time children are on various sites, games, or shopping, and can be shut off when time limits are reached. Parental controls help provide natural accountability and teach lessons for stewardship without you policing and fighting to gain access to their devices.
- Make sure you are a contact on every site they are on. It will help you hold them accountable to what they post, while also alerting you to what other friends or peers may be posting to your child's accounts.
- Consider why you allow kids to have certain social media accounts or online access. Do they really need it? Is it a necessary way of communicating with clubs, schools, or youth groups? What are the pros, cons, dangers, and benefits?
- Consider healthy lifestyle standards you want to help young people establish. Be proactive in preventing kids from staying on devices all hours of the day or night, encourage habits for a good night's sleep, and set up standards that keep devices out of bedrooms and only used in common areas where anyone can walk by and see what they are working on. Make sure they are not taking devices with them where you can't supervise them—especially the bathroom.
- What is needed for one child may vary from another child. It is important to know what guiding principles and rules you establish for your home and when you want to adapt rules because it makes sense to do so for the needs of an individual or for a season of time. For example, one child may need an app so they can keep up with what is happening in

drama club, but another child may not. Maybe a teen needs to download a certain app for a senior trip, or a sports season, but then it can be removed.

- When helping young people decide how to handle their time on smartphones, tablets, and other electronic devices, train them to avoid putting personal information online. As mentioned earlier, describe what information might be safe to post (first name, age, grade), and what is unwise to post (last name, address, phone numbers, where they attend school, etc.). Helping them understand how that information could be misused helps them begin to discern if what they are about to say is wise or unwise. Should they ever announce they are home alone? Is it wise to announce you will be going on vacation (and the house will be empty)?

- Explain that expressing or venting your feelings online is not only unwise but can have grave consequences. In a moment of anger, harsh things can be said that cause a chain reaction. Teach them that if they should not be saying something in front of a room full of students and teachers, they should not be saying it online either.

There is blatant and hidden danger in the world and we must learn that we cannot lean exclusively on our own understanding when navigating the hazardous landscape of technology. How much harder is it for tech-savvy young people to mistakenly believe they know how to safely traverse the digital world, especially since they are often more knowledgeable of technology trends than their parents.

Kids who are given the skills of distinguishing good from evil and who are raised to think, evaluate, and wisely respond to trouble will not lean on their own understanding. We can feel confident when they face hard things like social media and other online struggles that our kids will know how to acknowledge the Lord in all they do, and this will lead them down straight paths.

CHAPTER 19

Pornography and Sexting

"The eye is the lamp of the body. So, if your eye is healthy, your whole body will be full of light, but if your eye is bad, your whole body will be full of darkness. If then the light in you is darkness, how great is the darkness." Matthew 6:22–23

Young people are drawn to what is tantalizing. Sadly, we live in a culture that is sex-saturated and glorifies a grossly distorted view of sexuality. Children or teens may be initially repulsed or shocked upon first exposure to pornography or other sexually explicit content, but they will also be tempted and enticed. Curiosity about sex may draw young people into viewing imagery that will not give them an accurate picture of how God created sex but rather corrupt their understanding of what is good. This also confuses young people with a false sense of what is normal in real life relationships.

Whether it begins because of natural curiosity, outright lust, or the manipulation of another person, it is easier than ever for our children to be drawn into an addictive, destructive relationship with pornography. Not only is it easily accessible, but there are wicked people who will actively pursue your children and expose them to pornography in order to corrupt and abuse them.

Long-Term Effects of Unchecked Exposure to Pornography

Kids who are exposed to pornography will naturally begin to indulge in sexual fantasies. When this goes unchecked, they will often seek avenues to act upon their fantasies. And while everyone may struggle with sexual sin or temptation, what makes pornography insidious is that it takes over the mind and heart and captures their affections. It builds strong roots that shape your child's character and affections. Much research has been done to show the ways pornography has a negative impact on young people. A quick Google search on the topic will show you the alarming statistics of the long-term effects it can have if left unaddressed.

One such study states that "Excessive media use, particularly where the content is violent, gender-stereotyped, and/or sexually explicit, skews children's worldview, increases high-risk behaviors, and alters their capacity for successful and sustained human relationships."[19]

Teenagers who struggle with pornography addiction struggle with more than sex; they also begin to struggle with relationships. Pornography confuses kids to think that what they see online is what healthy dating or relationships should look like and how they should perform. It objectifies and transforms sex into something far less than what it was created to be—it takes something relational and turns it into something degrading and self-gratifying. Young people get taken in by an artificial world that looks glamorous, where they are the center of attention and where they feel desirable and wanted. Make no mistake—our children are actively being seduced by the pornography industry, and the results are extremely harmful.

Consider what this secular study on how pornography harms young people has to say:

> Studies on sexual content and violence in the media indicate that youth accept, learn from, and may emulate behaviors portrayed in the media as normative, attractive, and without risk. This is particularly concerning in light of the amount of pornographic materials that portray violence towards women. Past studies of the content of pornography concluded that the typical sexual script focuses on the sexual desires and prowess of men. A 2010 study of 50 popular pornographic

films suggests that popular pornography contains high levels of physical and verbal aggression. The study found that only 10.2% of pornographic scenes did not contain an aggressive act. Physical aggression occurred in 88.2% of scenes and verbal aggression in 48.7%. Men committed 70.3% of all aggressive acts and 94.4% of aggression was directed towards women.[20]

For some, pornography feeds on a sense of power and control. Consider the young man who feels powerless, or weak, or unaccepted. He enters into the world of pornography and is told he is desirable, masculine, and in control. He is encouraged to express himself and his urges and he feels powerful, in control of his world. It begins to shape the way he views the opposite sex, allowing him to fantasize, degrading and objectifying the women in his life so he feels stronger and more dominant.

Sexual fantasy feeds many corrupt attitudes and behaviors that all tend to be self-centered, driven by escapism and pleasure, providing an altered sense of reality that deeply impacts friendships and relationships. Rather than learning to work through tough relational moments, kids learn to escape into a fantasy world where they feel they can control their relationships. Often this is done by dominance.

Parents Must Step In

Psalm 119:37 says this: "Turn my eyes from looking at worthless things; and give me life in your ways." What seems to provide momentary pleasure is really worthless and empty. It leads to death and distraction. Your son and daughter need your help making sense out of their experiences and the rampant temptations around them. They need you to understand their struggle and give them hope and a way to escape the temptation and the lure of worthless things.

Ask them what they think this verse means by "worthless things." Then follow up by discussing ways you too might be tempted to look at or pursue worthless things. It helps when we show our kids that we are all tempted to look to the wrong things for the wrong type of fulfillment or gratification. Ask them to share the ways they are tempted. Share that you know pursuing sexual purity is a struggle for us all, but when we ask God to give wisdom, he reorients our hearts and our affections to reflect his perfect design.

Every child, teen, parent, and home is different. The way each of us struggles or is tempted may vary, but the themes are often the same. Look for ways to draw out your children's thoughts, feelings, and struggles. Then point them to hope, that God both understands and sympathizes with them, and has promised to provide a way of escape.

Below are some practical suggestions and principles for talking to your teen about pornography:

- Be proactive in shaping your teenagers views about sex, sexuality, gender, and godly relationships.
- Cultivate and pursue open conversations about the temptations of pornography, as well as the damage it does.
- Prepare them for ways they might be exposed to graphic imagery. It may be through peers, movies, online gaming, or predators pursuing them online.
- Teach them how you would like them to respond when they see graphic images and what steps they should take (deleting the image right away, shutting off the device, walking away, etc.) Acknowledge that sometimes they might be exposed to pornography due to no fault of their own. Assure them they will not be in trouble and help them think through how to respond and rebuff such attempts to be drawn in.
- Remind them that if they have intentionally delved into pornography, God offers abundant grace and forgiveness. Regardless of mistakes they might make, they can turn from temptation and start fresh.
- Identify mature adults they can go to for help or talk to when they are struggling. Acknowledge that sometimes they may be afraid to come to you.

Encourage your teenager to develop a personal relationship with the Lord. There is no stronger safeguard than a child having a deep conviction and sense of right and wrong. When a child develops a love for God, they will be grounded in God's ways and flourish.

As mentioned above, God knows our struggles. Scripture says we have a high priest who can sympathize with our weakness (Hebrews 4:15) and who also provides a way of escape when we need it (1 Corinthians 10:13). Be a beacon of understanding, knowledge, hope, and compassion. Our kids will struggle. They will wrestle with temptation, and they need to see we understand and can offer them wisdom and help.

Reiterate to your teens you know they are not perfect and they may struggle, stumble, and regret their choices. Let them know you will support them and forgiveness is freely given. Pointing them to the Lord in the midst of struggle reminds them where hope and help is found. Remind them that the Lord's mercies are new every morning (Lamentations 3:22–23).

Sexting

Sexting, the sending of nude pictures via text or social media was most likely not a part of your life growing up, but it is certainly part of your child's world. If your child has any device, they are at risk of being sent or being asked to send sexualized photos. Sexting has all the dangers and perils of pornography (objectification and self-gratification), and the long-term ramifications can be explosive.

Sexting will often start in the context of a boyfriend/girlfriend relationship. Young men will often pressure their girlfriends to send pictures of themselves naked or dressed inappropriately. Teenage girls will feel the pressure and may want to please or impress their boyfriend. Now imagine that young man sending that picture to all his friends to impress them with how hot his girlfriend is. Before she knows it, her picture is being forwarded without consent around the school with no ability to stop it. It ends up on social media and she is bullied, called all kinds of crude names, and is mocked by peers.

Personal Risks of Sexting

Another all-too-common scenario for sexting is when teenagers break up. In this case, the photos are used and made public to exact revenge against an ex. Teens are embarrassed, ashamed, afraid to go out in public, and cannot get away from the fact that their nude image is both now public and permanently part of a digital footprint. If a teenager applies for a job or applies for colleges and their name or image is searched, these images can resurface, even years down the road.

Teach your teens that they will leave a digital foot print everywhere they go, and once their images are out there on social media or other sites, it is difficult to get rid of them. Teenagers need help understanding the humiliation, guilt, and despair that comes from such activity.

Sexting often turns into cyberbullying. An inappropriate, private picture shared between two people easily turns into public mocking and consequences. If that isn't dangerous enough, consider the many ways your teenager becomes vulnerable to the grooming of predators. Sexual predators will often request photos of a child or teenager. They will then use those photos to blackmail and force or coerce teenagers into sexual favors. Some will take such photos and post them on child pornography websites and exploit the images. Help your teen understand that an unwise decision to send a naked picture can have life-altering repercussions. Many girls have fallen into depression, anxiety, and have even become suicidal over their images being used and misused.

The Legal Ramifications of Sexting

It is also worth noting that most teenagers are unaware of the laws around sexting. In many states, having a naked picture of an underage child constitutes child pornography, and the one who has the picture can be held criminally liable. It does not matter that your teenage son was sent that picture by his buddy. If your son is found with a nude photo of another teenager, he can face criminal charges.

It is illegal to send sexually explicit photos of any individual under the age of eighteen. You could be criminally charged if you take a nude, semi-nude, or sexually graphic photo of an underage individual, even if it is of yourself or if it is with that person's consent. If a friend or anyone else sends you a photo or video and it is found on your device, you can be held legally accountable. If your teenager forwards a photo or video that was sent to them of an underage child, they can be held legally liable. All of these acts fall under a code for child pornography and have serious penalties.

All of these reasons are why teaching your young people to have character and respect for others is so foundational to helping safeguard them against these dangers. A child that is raised to look at people and treat them with dignity will be less likely to get caught up in these destructive situations. Even good kids are tempted and make bad decisions in the heat of the moment. Don't assume because you had this conversation once that your children are prepared for the challenges before them. It is vital that we keep the lines of communication open and are always inviting our kids to talk to us about these things.

Suggestions for Talking to Your Kids about Sexting

- Have an open-door policy with your kids. Encourage conversation and bring up the hard topics for them.
- Educate your children about sexting: what it is, why people fall into the temptation, and how they can avoid it.
- Assume that your child will one day be presented with a request or will be sent a nude photo. Talk through how they should handle it (deleting it immediately, talk to you, etc.). Remind them they should never save it, pass it onto another individual, or participate in a dialogue about the photo.
- Be very clear about what the laws are and how it could impact them should they not listen to wisdom.

- Remind them that people are not always who they say they are, and once they send any type of photo or personal information, it is possible for it to be misused.
- If your teenager receives any sexually explicit communication from an adult, have them immediately go to you or another trustworthy adult and report it to the authorities.
- Be willing to talk about the reasons kids cave in to these requests. Talk about identity, peer pressure, the desire to be accepted, and the temptations that come with these desires.

These are serious conversations to have about serious issues that have serious consequences. That's why it's important for you to always affirm your love for your children. Remind them that you know they will make mistakes and struggle, and you will be there to help them. Take the time to remind them of God's love for them and that even (especially) in the midst of trouble, God will be with them and his right hand will hold them fast (Psalm 139:10).

CHAPTER 20

Alcohol Abuse, Drugs, and Smoking/Vaping

"Or do you not know that your body is a temple of the Holy Spirit within you, whom you have from God? You are not your own, for you were bought with a price. So glorify God in your body."
1 Corinthians 6:19–20

When children become teenagers, they begin to face temptations and situations that they may have previously been sheltered from: exposure to pornography, the struggles of a suicidal or abused friend, sexual opportunities, and/or access to drugs and alcohol. For many teens, these issues are hitting them for the first time and without proactive preparation, they will often cave to either the temptations of peer pressure. As parents, it's important to have conversations with your children from a young age, as we have already discussed, to teach them that God created them and we take care of our bodies to honor him and be good stewards of what he has given to us. The overarching principle when talking with your children about activities that could harm them is stewardship. In everything, we are called to glorify God, and that includes how we care for our bodies and what choices we make about what to put into it.

Schools have historically worked hard to prevent kids from starting to smoke and to use drugs and alcohol. Scary testimonies of the lifelong effects of drug use or videos of drunk driving car accidents can have momentary shock value, but when the shock wears off and teens see their peers having fun vaping, doing drugs, or drinking without any immediate repercussions, they begin to doubt that there is a real risk. Teens are still developing emotionally and cognitively; they lack maturity and insight. They are notoriously poor at judging or accessing risk, not to mention that they see themselves as invincible.

And though it seems that kids mostly get the message about the dangers of drug and alcohol abuse, as well as the health risks of smoking and vaping, they may be hearing false information from their peers. When they don't see any immediate problems, they doubt all the warnings. Peers often present these activities as innocuous. However, they are dangerous. Kids should not drink alcohol or use any drug or nicotine product. Recent science raises concerns about the adverse effects of marijuana and nicotine on adolescent development, not to mention that there are a wide variety of other toxins being consumed in things like e-cigarette vapor.[21]

Discipling Your Kids Through Temptations

Ask your teens what they know about drugs, smoking, or vaping and what they think about it. Talk to them about the dangers—but don't focus only on the repercussions and consequences. Broaden the conversation to be about the bigger issues involved, like facing temptations and following Christ. See this as another opportunity to walk alongside and disciple them in a world full of enticements that threaten to consume them. Whether it is pornography, alcohol, drugs, or any other temptation, let them know you understand the pressures they face, because you face them, too. Once they know you understand, you will win a voice in their life. Identify with how hard it can be to live in this world and not give in to what is tempting. Sympathize with their struggle; they will feel heard and understood.

Here are a few ways to disciple your kids through these temptations:

- Connect them to God who understands their struggle. Remind them often of his compassion. (Hebrews 4:15–16)
- Young people need direction and help to live self-controlled lives. Model self-discipline yourself. (Titus 2:12)
- Instill in them that even if something seems permissible (legal, acceptable, not dangerous), it does not mean it is good—or good for you. (1 Corinthians 6:12)
- Remind them that God can provide a way out from tempting situations (1 Corinthians 10:13–14). Remind them that when they are caught in a struggle, God can deliver them. Then take the next step and provide options and help. For example: call a friend, reach out to a mentor, shut off the internet, ask for accountability, etc.
- Be available and accessible when they are struggling. (Psalm 50:15)
- Remind them that there is always grace and forgiveness waiting for each of us. Point them to the free offer of forgiveness through Jesus when they sin. (1 John 1:8–9)

Because we are faced with similar struggles to conform or seek acceptance, we can offer honest sympathy for their struggles—we face temptation too. We have an opportunity to show compassion and offer wisdom from our own hard lessons learned. Our kids also need Scripture to be made relevant in their lives and parents are the greatest resource God can use to do that.

What are some practical ways you could offer help for the specific temptation they are facing? Again, role-playing the scenarios they may find themselves in is one of the best ways to prepare them. Help them find words to respond with if they are offered a substance. Simple phrases that they feel most comfortable saying are always best. Things like, "I'm not into that" or "No, I don't do that stuff—don't ask again" can be short and simple ways to rebuff such pressure. Encourage and praise them when you see them taking a stand.

Every story you hear, every failure, and every conversation when they share their heart is an opportunity for you to impart wisdom and good discernment to your children. Rather than lecturing them when they make unwise decisions, use conversations as an opportunity to help them grow in wisdom. Asking good questions is often far better than instruction. For example, if your teenager shares with you about all the destructive things his coworkers did over the weekend, it's easy to respond by simply saying, "that's terrible." But, it would be far better to ask some simple questions like, "What were you thinking as you heard them talk?" "How are you processing what they said?" "Did that make you feel like you were missing out?" "What do you think you would have done if you were in that situation?"

Such questions help you know how your children think about and evaluate the people around them. It gives you insight into where they might be tempted or where they could glamorize the lives of others. It gives you a window into their hearts and helps you know how to converse well with them about the issues they are facing. It also makes them feel heard and understood. It prevents them from feeling that you are there to simply judge, lecture, and condemn. Instead, it shows that you care about how they think and feel.

By listening well and taking the time to really talk with them, you are sending a message that their opinion is valued when you listen to them and let them express their thoughts. We all know that when we feel somebody values our opinion it is far easier to hear their thoughts and receive input.

It's easy for parents to get sidetracked by fear when their teenagers share some of what's happening in their lives—but work at being open. Ask God for the grace to remember that he loves your children more than you do and that he is the one that will provide a way of escape for the temptations they face. Fear, as we have discussed already, is paralyzing. Faith gives us the opportunity to take small steps of love toward our children by listening and helping them evaluate their world with wisdom and discernment.

CHAPTER 21

Navigating Mental Health Struggles

"It is the LORD who goes before you. He will be with you; he will not
leave you or forsake you. Do not fear or be dismayed."
Deuteronomy 31:8

When teenagers struggle with their mental health, it's often hard to
know why and how to help. Their difficulties could be due to a variety of reasons: harm done to them, choices they have made, inherent
struggles and brokenness, and learned behavior (just to name a few).
In any struggle, we want our kids to know they are not alone. The
One who created them always goes with them, goes before them, and
is in the midst of their battles. They also need to know that regardless of what they are facing, we will support them. They desperately
need mature, loving voices in their lives to help them navigate their
emotional struggles.

Staying in Tune with Your Child's Mental Health

Teens are increasingly facing mental health issues. They are likely to
face (or have peers who are facing) anything from anxiety, depression,
suicide, identity issues, hopelessness, addiction, and more. Parents
who regularly talk with their children, pursue them, and engage with
them are far more likely to pick up on these kinds of struggles. A teen

who is committed to keeping things from their parents will find ways to do so, but it will be much harder if parents are proactive and in tune with their kids' lives. Talk to your kids about recognizing when they're feeling sad or depressed or might be struggling with body image issues or an eating disorder. Again, the more you talk to them about these things, the less fearful and stigmatizing it will seem if they come to you with their struggles.

As a parent, pay attention to your instincts when you are concerned. Parents and other close mentors likely know their teens better than anyone else. Very few people will be as committed to knowing and understanding a teen's mental health then a parent or close adult. They spend the most time and energy on their relationship, they have the most conversations with them, so they will also be among the first to notice a change in behavior.

Wise adults intuitively read a child's face, body language, and silences. Parents often pick up on signs that something is amiss because they have spent years observing their children. It is discernment born out of multitudes of moments watching how their kids respond to moments of sadness, frustration, hurt, anger, and joy. It comes from thousands of big and small moments and life experiences parents have lived with their children. It is noticing what looks like "normal" reactions from their children and things that seem out of the norm. While parents are the ones to most quickly pick up on signs that something is amiss, any close mentor or family member who knows the teen well can also be attuned to changes in how a teen responds to moments of sadness, frustration, hurt, anger, and joy.

This does not mean you can catch every abnormality in their behavior or mood, nor does it mean you always know the reasons why a teenager may be "off." It simply means you often sense something before you are able to articulate the reasons why—and you shouldn't be afraid to take notice. It also doesn't mean a parent or youth worker should take the blame for missing a teen's behavior. Kids who really want to hide or deceive can do so. No matter how in tune you are, you could miss what they've kept deeply hidden.

If you suspect your teen is at risk, do not hesitate to get help. Get the teen talking, especially to trustworthy adults. Whether a counselor, youth leader, mentor, parent, or a trusted adult, pursue people who will speak into this teen's life. If you believe your child is in immediate risk, call 911, get them to a hospital, and get them professional help.[22]

When Your Child's Friends Are Struggling

It's also important to talk to your teenagers about what to do if they are struggling emotionally— or if their friends open up and admit they are struggling. Sometimes your teen may be doing well, but as they interact with a peer who is struggling, they find themselves adopting similar emotional struggles.

Friends may open up to your child about feeling depressed or even suicidal, but they may ask your child not to share that information with anyone. Your teen will want to be a good friend but will feel overwhelmed with helping or knowing what to do. Your teen may find that in order to connect with a peer, they take on their struggles as their own or begin to empathize too much with a peer. We see this happen in issues such as self-injury and suicide. Teens begin to influence each other in negative thought patterns and behaviors.

What should they do in those moments? Talk at length with your child about what it looks like to be a good friend and how they can know whether something is serious enough to bring in adult intervention.

Here are some questions you can ask to help evaluate the severity of their struggles (or a friend's struggle):

- Do you feel unsafe? Discuss what type of things might make them and/or a friend feel unsafe. For example, are they hurting themselves or are they avoiding food or medical care?
- Are they engaged in destructive behaviors (cutting, drugs or alcohol, etc.)? Do they seem to talk at length about guns, wanting to kill animals, or harm others? Are their behaviors increasing in severity or frequency?

- Are they willing to seek help?
- Are any mature adults in their life aware of what is happening?
- Are they being bullied, and have you witnessed it? Has anybody been able to effectively intervene? How is it impacting them and are they sharing with anyone?
- Are they withdrawing from normal activities, giving away their possessions, making statements online or publicly about wanting to die or life being meaningless? Are any of these things increasing in frequency?
- Do they have a support system and how helpful are those individuals?
- *Trust your instincts.*

Help your son and daughter grow in courage to share what they are feeling and doing, even when they know others may be upset or angry with them. Talk about how they may not appreciate it in the moment, but when help and resources are given, and they feel a renewed sense of hope and support, they may even thank you. Even when they aren't thankful, they can be confident that what was done was for their good, even when they were unable to see it themselves.

Here is where helping your kids understand what real support looks like, giving them the courage and boldness to make hard decisions that will be unpopular in the moment, but are wise, loving, and will rescue them. It also raises their expectations of how to respond to their friends. It becomes a win-win when we are willing to have these conversations with our teenagers.

If your child has a friend who is struggling, discourage your teenagers from trying to rescue their friends on their own. There are many kids who feel like it is their job to function as a counselor or therapist for one of their friends, to be available twenty-four hours a day if their friend is hurting, or they feel the weight and pressure of resolving their friend's struggles or bearing their burdens. What young person has the wisdom and insight to be able to help one of their own peers through hard, broken places? Many adults feel ill-equipped to do so. It is a burden they were never meant to bear, nor do they have the resources to effectively intervene in a friend's experience. Instead, point them to skilled people who can help. Perhaps this is a guidance counselor at school, a trusted adult at school, or another parent. Your child's best role is to simply be a caring friend without taking on the responsibility of resolving their problems.

Consider talking through these scenarios with your kids:

- What would you do if a friend of yours said they felt suicidal? (Option: Go with them to one or two caring adults and share how they are feeling.)
- How should you respond if one of your classmates posted on social media that they were selling drugs? (Involve a parent, adult, or guidance counselor, talk to your friend, and express your concern.)
- If a friend confided they were hearing voices and the voices were telling them to harm someone, what would you say or do? (Ask them to share this with a parent or adult, offer to go with them, continue to be a good friend.)
- If a friend admitted to having an eating disorder, how would you respond? (Express concern, offer support, invite in mature influences—discuss who that might be.)
- Have you ever known a friend or classmate who struggles with depression? What do you notice about them? What could you say or what would you want to say to them? (Talk about how to encourage, offer hope, and get help from a mature, caring adult.)
- If you thought a peer was in serious trouble, who would you go to? (Who do you trust? Who might be closest to your friend? What type of trouble might it be?)
- What could make teenagers feel more comfortable going to their parents or an adult? (A guarantee of support, not being in trouble, listening well, etc.)

- Who would you go to if you ever felt depressed, struggled with an eating disorder, or wanted to harm yourself? (Give them room to have a variety of good choices and offer them people you would trust to help.)
- Have you ever been worried for one of your friends? Why? (Talk through signs and behavior that they have learned to evaluate that tell them someone is in trouble.)

Make up your own questions, listen, and ask more questions. Your kids will talk if you take time and show patience. Both teens and parents need help making sense of their experience and finding hope in the midst of an upsetting battle for a child's well-being. A godly, wise perspective gives you the ability to remember what is true, what is momentary, and what is eternal. It shapes what you do with your heartache and emotions, and reminds you where your confidence truly lies. It also helps you point your teen to hope and the one who will carry and equip them in their struggle, as well as struggles they are exposed to by their peers.

In a resource I wrote about teens and suicide, I remind parents:

Life includes a multitude of joys and much heartbreak. Christian homes are not immune to the trials of this world; they fall on believers and unbelievers alike. However, God promises to deliver us from the evil of it. A godly hope positions us in the center of God's will. It reminds us that we live for something better than what is temporary. It gives us a vision for eternity. That means I can trust God with a teen's struggles as well as my own.[23]

Your teens' (and their friends') mental health struggles are not outside of God's care and concern. God is watching and keeping them and will be their help and yours in the trouble you are facing with them.

CHAPTER 22

Safety Skills for Growing Independence

"When I was a child, I spoke like a child, I thought like a child, I
reasoned like a child. When I became a man, I gave up childish ways."
1 Corinthians 13:11

As your child enters older adolescence they often believe they have
arrived at full maturity and are ready to teach us a thing or two.
At the same time, we are still reminding them to brush their teeth,
pick up their room, and eat more than Doritos and Lucky Charms.
Greater independence and autonomy does not immediately equate to
maturity and wisdom. It requires ongoing discipleship and equipping
so that our young people begin to reason and respond maturely.

It is our responsibility to not let up on our active pursuit and
influence, even when our teens think they no longer need us. This
is a time to press in even more to build relationship with them. We
move in to earn their respect, gain their trust, and demonstrate that
we are still a relevant and much-needed support. This is not done with
the goal to control them, but to maintain relationship. We choose to
come alongside them and offer to be a guide and ongoing influence.
As we do, we pray for the Spirit to guide them and to give them listening ears to God and his Word.

We have spent a great deal of time talking about helping our kids
evaluate behavior and choices, and discern right from wrong, to grow

in wisdom and discernment. We also, as parents, must evaluate and discern the behavior of our teens and young adults. We evaluate their behavior and choices, passions and pursuits, and we watch to see if they are growing and maturing in the ways of wisdom. We pray for them and look for opportunities to steer them.

Do you feel you have laid a foundation of equipping your child with safety skills? Does your teen know how to evaluate the behavior of those around them? If not, please feel free to go back through the earlier sections of this book and make a commitment to teach your kids to evaluate behavior, not character. The key principle your teenagers need to remember from earlier in the book is that strangers are not dangerous—dangerous people are. They need to be able to evaluate whether what a person is asking them to do is good, right or wrong, or even questionable. They also need to know who to call if they need help.

Most teens and young adults presume they will know if they are in danger. Yet they often lack the maturity or the foresight to see potential hazards when it comes to a variety of safety situations. We can and must instill confidence and independence in our kids while also helping them avoid or remove themselves from dangerous or risky situations.

Because your child is now more independent does not mean they are less vulnerable. Teenagers are vulnerable in ways that are different from a child. At least with young children, they are rarely unsupervised, while teenagers are often unsupervised. Not only are they left to their own devices and to the wise or unwise choices they may make; they are also subject to the wise or foolish choices their peers make. Whether it is the behavior of their friends, a boyfriend/ girlfriend, teachers, coaches, youth leaders, older siblings, or other relatives, your kids must be willing to evaluate and rebuff anyone they feel is acting inappropriately.

Questions for Teenagers to Ask

This is a lot of responsibility for them! But if you have laid a foundation of helping them to know how to evaluate someone's behavior, they will be able to ask the right questions. When someone asks them to do something, they should be asking: Is it good and right? Or is it uncomfortable, wrong, immoral, or even illegal? If you've raised your teen to pay attention to behavior and have given them freedom to refuse anyone, even adults, who tell them to do something that is wrong or inappropriate, they will navigate a variety of potentially harmful situations much more easily.

Teach them to pay attention to what makes them uncomfortable and evaluate why. They may evaluate something as innocuous or innocent, but later should it come up again, they will be able to build on their concern and pay attention. Is someone frequently flattering them, giving them gifts, or showering them with attention? If so, teach them to assess why. Teach them that it is a red flag if adults seek to spend time alone with them, particularly if it is away from public view. Perhaps a coach they desperately want to impress begins to make them uncomfortable with their displays of affection. Maybe a youth group leader or volunteer begins to shower them with special attention and opportunities. Maybe it's their best friend's older brother or cousin who consistently calls them a prude because they won't smoke pot with him.

Help Them Identify Safe People

With your teenager, identify two or three safe, mature adults you would want your teenagers to go to if they ever felt they needed to talk to someone and they couldn't come to you. Encourage them that regardless of what is wrong, you would be happy for them to go to these people and they would not be in trouble. Talk through the potential ways they might seek help from these adults, perhaps if they're feeling peer pressure or sexual temptation from a dating relationship, maybe they were exposed to drugs or smoking, or maybe they're struggling with a life choice or decision and they don't know how to share it with you as a parent.

Many kids have only their own peer group to rely on as a source of counsel. You want to do everything you can to ensure your kids have wiser mature people available when needed. When a teenager recognizes some behavior or situation as wrong or inappropriate, it can feel like the moment has passed or the time to act has already passed. Assure your teens that you would still want to hear about their experience and help them process it. Whether you wish they had come to you sooner or responded differently, thank them for telling you about it and being willing to be honest with you.

Assure them of your love for them and your desire to always be able to talk about the hard things. You may think that I am saying this over and over again, but I am not sure I can emphasize it enough. It is important to encourage and affirm teenagers even in the moment you wish they did something different. We underestimate how hard it is for our young people to share things that they think will get them in trouble, are embarrassed about, or fear will disappoint us. You need to encourage and affirm your love for them in any given situation so the next time they will come to you again (perhaps even sooner). If they receive criticism or a lecture, you can be quite certain they'll hesitate coming to you next time.

Code Words

Earlier in this book, we discussed the option for code words, safe words, and other ways a child can communicate to a parent the need for assistance when they find themselves in unexpected situations. Now let's consider ways this could be helpful for teens.

I want my teens to be strong enough in their character to be able to stand up to negative behavior, and I will work to help them do so. However, I also understand the nature of peer pressure, unexpected surprises, and the many confusing events teens can find themselves in and not know what to do. We want our kids to "stand up for what's right," but it is unrealistic to think that such situations will always be clearcut.

Our kids can find themselves in uncomfortable or unsafe scenarios due to no fault of their own, and they may not be prepared, quick enough on their feet, or assertive enough to know how to get out of it. Sometimes it is due to foolish decisions they've made. For example, consider the teenage boy who decides to jump in the car with his friends after school and go for a ride, knowing that his parents would not be okay with it. While they are driving, one of his friends opens up a bottle of vodka and begins passing it around. Your son is uncomfortable and knows it is illegal to be driving with an open container—not to mention they are all minors. He feels uncomfortable questioning his peers and uncertain how to get out of it. He is also aware if he calls or texts his parents they will be upset to find that he is in a car with his friends without their permission. What does he do? Who can he call? And if he's afraid to let his parents know that he needs help getting out of the situation, what could he do discreetly so as to avoid an even more questionable situation with his peers?

Having a code word or phrase can be really helpful for kids in this situation—something that tells them mom or dad will be there or be their excuse to get them out of the predicament they are in without question and without hesitation. Consider some examples you could give your teen/young adult:

- Tell them if they are ever in an uncomfortable situation and they are afraid, they should text you, "Dad, I forgot to take my medication." You will know this will be a sign to ask, "Do we need to bring it to you?" This is code for, "Do you want me to come get you?" The teen can answer yes or no.
- If your teens need to leave a questionable situation on their own, but they need an excuse, they could say, "My mom says there is an emergency at home and told me to leave right away." Or, "Sorry guys, I have to check in with my parents, you know how parents are—if I don't check in, they will come looking for me." Then your child calls or texts you to let you know what they need.
- Maybe it is a simple phrase, like a movie quote, "Your killing me, Smalls" or maybe it is one word your family would never normally use like "Nutter Butter." Whatever it might be, make it easy to remember and accessible enough to alert you to the need for intervention.

We have also given our kids permission to make us the "bad guys" or to use us as an excuse for getting out of the situation. "Sorry, guys, my mom just texted me that I need to come home." When they are not brave or assertive enough to do so, I want to be willing to take on the blame or responsiblity to provide a way of escape for them. No questions asked (or very little) in the moment. The goal is simply to help them get out of the unsafe scenario. It might be tempting to ask a lot of questions, grill them on why they are where they are or who they are with and how they got there, but try to withhold those questions or your kids will avoid calling you in the midst of peril. Of course, we will always circle back around and process it with them. It is necessary to talk through the event later, but in the moment, I want to guarantee their safety and give them ways to get out of a scary or dangerous situation.

Public Safety Skills for Emerging Independence

Not too long ago, our college age daughter was taking a break from work at a local daycare. She decided to drive to a local coffee shop and sit in her car to relax and get away from work for a brief period of time. After about twenty minutes, she decided it was time to go. She turned on her engine and slowly began to back out of her parking spot. It was then that she saw an older gentleman approaching her car.

She was rolling up her window when she paused, uncertain if perhaps she had a flat tire or something was wrong with the car. When he approached her window, he threw something into her lap, looked at her and said, "I've been watching you for a while. You have pretty eyes." He then turned around and walked away as she rolled up her window. When she looked down, she saw he had thrown a fifty-dollar bill on her lap. It wasn't until she got back to work and began thinking about it a bit more that the discomfort and potential danger of the situation hit her. It was broad daylight, a sunny day, and beautiful weather on a busy section of town. There had been no reason at all for a nineteen-year-old girl to worry about her safety. Yet this very uncomfortable, inappropriate exchange happened and she was caught off guard. This is a young woman who has heard her parents repeatedly talk to her about safety, being cautious, and evaluating people's behavior. And here was a good example of a situation that unfolded within less than a minute or two, caught her off guard, and shook her up after she had time to process the facts.

It is a prime example of how we can teach our young people to do everything right and they will still need to know how to respond to unsafe people who do inappropriate or unsafe things. We will never quite know if she was ever truly unsafe, but what we do know is that somebody approached her without permission, made unwanted comments and advances, and left her feeling rattled.

After noticing what he did, I would have recommended she stop the car and call 911 right away and ask a police officer to show up. There is no guarantee what would've unfolded, but what we do know is an officer would've given that man a good talking to and would have certainly sent a message to him that she did not appreciate, nor would she tolerate what he did. Perhaps she could've even gone into the coffee shop and let somebody know what had happened so that they were on a lookout for this man as well. Regardless, it became a great teaching moment and opportunity to process what she did well, what she could do differently in the future, and how to think about unexpected situations like this.

Perhaps one of the hardest scenarios to help your young person navigate is when somebody approaches them. It could be a sales person, an older woman or gentleman looking for directions, or it could be somebody with the sinister intent of testing the waters to see how open or naive your teenager will be.

When your teenagers are approached by people they may or may not know, consider the posture you want them to have. One way I think about this is to encourage them to be alert and consider why someone is approaching them. It is wise to be cautious.

I want them to consider where they are and think about what the potential risks might be. For example, if they are alone at night, walking to their car, you want them to be more cautious and aware. If someone approached them, I might encourage them to tell the person not to get any closer and speak to them from across the car. However, if my teenager is in a crowded amusement park and their friends are with them, they could be free to stop and listen to what the person has to say, then evaluate the behavior.

Public safety is important for your teens and young adults, no matter the age. If they're on a hike, what would they do if they're in trouble or needed help? If their car breaks down, what would you encourage them to do, and would that differ if it breaks down at night versus in broad daylight, in a congested shopping area or a secluded highway?

What if your teenager is offered a ride home by somebody they are acquainted with? In what instances would you want them to accept or decline the ride?

Things that can seem innocent and innocuous might be a test to see if your son or daughter can be manipulated. A young person who is regularly given the skills to evaluate and pay attention will notice it much sooner and respond before the stakes get too high.

As you can see, this all takes constant conversation. Evaluation and discernment skills don't easily translate over from one situation to the next without a lot of practicing, asking a lot of *what ifs*, and equipping your kids to test, evaluate, and notice things. The more they do this, the more it will become as natural as breathing. They won't have to be anxious, because responding wisely will become instinctive.

For example, a teen going shopping or hanging out at the local park may be very relaxed and enjoying their time with their peer group. A skillful teen will also be aware of their surroundings. They observe who is at the park and whether anyone is approaching in a threatening way. Is the group of guys over on the basketball court having fun and being lighthearted, or are they passing out drugs and acting suspiciously?

Your teenage girls can go shopping together at the mall and sit at a food court enjoying themselves and laughing. But they also can scan the room and be aware of the lovely older couple two tables down and notice three men who are consistently glancing over at them as they eat. Your daughters are not fearful; they're in a public place, but they also look around to notice whether there are security guards or other adults they can turn to should these men make them uncomfortable.

These are skills every teenager can exercise naturally that won't cause them to live in a constant state of worry. Instead, they are more perceptive and aware. It makes them confident that they can navigate hard things and know what to do should they be alone.

Draw examples from real-life stories you know about or have seen on the news. This demonstrates to your teens that these are real life issues and you are not simply a paranoid parent who sees danger where there is none. Talking these things over with your kids helps them think about what they would do and how they would choose to respond and helps you direct the conversation in ways that gives them ideas and solutions should it ever happen to them.

When Alone or Traveling

Most teenagers love independence, especially when they begin driving. Many of us can remember the first time we were able to take the car out on our own to go to the mall, run an errand, or spend time with a friend. Independence and being out on their own will be a natural part of our teenagers growing up. We want to equip them to do so safely.

Another mark of independence is leaving your teen alone for the evening, the day, or a weekend. Do you discuss what they can and can't do? Besides not burning the house down or throwing wild parties, what other guidance do you offer? You may tell them to keep the doors locked, but think about other obvious safety tips your teens may not even think about. How often are kids online while their parents are gone and casually announce to someone that they are home alone? Maybe your daughter is on social media and announces, "Home alone tonight, so glad!"

Whether it's a friend who puts pressure on them to invite them over and sneak out, or an online observer with devious intentions, your teen has announced they are alone and unsupervised for several hours. You should be concerned. Many teenagers succumb to the pressure of inviting somebody over when their parents are gone. Sometimes they are aware they are allowing potential mischief, and sometimes, they're completely oblivious to the danger they have just invited in.

Having these types of conversations helps your teen know you aren't just out to prevent them from having fun, but you want to keep them safe. Make the most of news stories and other actual accounts where things turned tragic for a teen who put themselves in harm's way while their parents were out of the house.

It is imperative that you brainstorm with all your kids on what to do if they are home alone and various situations unfold: a fire starts, a stranger knocks on the door, a neighbor or friend stops by, a burglar tries to enter, a professional shows up saying they have an appointment and need access to the home, etc. Help them think through what they can and should do in each situation. We often tell our kids that if they are home alone and someone comes to the door saying they have an appointment, our kids always have permission to turn them away—even if it was true and there was an appointment. If it was our fault for forgetting, not preparing them, or changing the appointment, we would never be mad at them for our mistake. We want them to have the ability to say no, ignore a phone call or doorbell, and value safety first.

Help your kids value safety over politeness. I'd be hard-pressed to want my kids to appear rude, but when it comes to safety, I would much rather my daughter be perceived as rude when a man is approaching her than to be perceived as an easy target. This is true of all my children, male or female, I want them to be safe even if it means they appear temporarily rude to someone who is trying to help them.

Encourage your teenager to be alert when they are alone. When out alone in public, be careful when someone approaches them. There may be a good reason for it, but don't hesitate to take a cautious posture. This means keeping a healthy distance, asking someone to step back, keeping a window rolled up or only cracked when they approach your car, and making sure you are in front of a waiter, store clerk, or another person who can help if needed.

It is okay, and often wise to say no or tell someone to stop when being approached. It is always best to be direct and clear. "Do not come any closer" is not rude; it is a safety precaution. A person may say, "Good grief, I was just trying to tell you that you have a flat tire." They may walk away mad or have a few choice words, but a person with no ill intentions will do just that—walk away. A person with ill intentions may keep trying to gain access and your fear of offending will be a tool they use to harm you.

Being cautious does not mean being fearful. It is helping young people to be more aware of their surroundings. Role-playing helps at every stage of development because new possibilities unfold that they haven't encountered before. Giving them a scenario to think about and talking through it before being put in a tense situation gives them an idea of how to proceed.

You can easily practice this while teaching your kids new things like how to drive. Be sure you have conversations about what to do if you get pulled over. What should your daughter do if pulled over by an unmarked officer or late at night? Who should she call or let know? Can she drive to a well-lit area first? What should your teen son do if he's in his car and someone approaches his window and asks him to roll it down to talk? What if they see someone in trouble late at night and they feel they should pull over to help? What would you advise? Should they get out of the car, call someone, or wait for an office to arrive?

More Practical Suggestions for Safety in Public

- Pay attention. It is wise to keep alert and avoid looking down, listening to music or appearing distracted. Whether someone intends harm, burglary, or something more devious, it is more appealing for them to approach and take advantage of a person who is distracted. Teach your kids to be aware of their surroundings.
- Keep visible. In public places and when alone at a park, stay places where others walk or drive by. If you cannot see others, they likely cannot see you should you need help.

- Let others know where you are and have regular check-ins. Should your teen get lost, break down in their car, or be in danger, the more people who know about their last known location, the more quickly help will arrive when needed. No one goes out assuming they will be stranded or in danger, but they will be thankful that people know their location when they need help. It could be a simple text, an app, or another way to help your child feel independent while also being safe.
- Encourage going places during daylight hours when possible.
- When using public transportation, consider who you sit next to and why. Do you feel safer next to a woman, a family, or someone older? Do you sit close to an employee or door, and why? Avoid compartments and places where you are alone or isolated.
- Don't keep your valuables sitting out for others to see. Whether in a car, on public transportation, or at a park, leaving electronics, wallets, or other valuables sitting out draws unwanted attention for those who are looking to rob you.
- In public places, congested areas, or when alone, encourage young women to carry their purses close to them, or keep valuables (like cash, credit cards, phone, etc.) in separate places. If mugged or robbed, they would not lose everything. Hide valuables in your car or trunk where others cannot see them.
- Think through travel arrangements and accommodations. When kids are traveling overnight, visiting a college, or traveling on a class trip, help them think through areas to avoid (such as shady restaurants or bars, unlit streets and shortcuts) and best ways to travel (good roads, easily accessible help, etc.).
- Avoid telling strangers, maybe even acquaintances, that you are alone. Be slow and cautious to trust people you just met.
- Be prepared, be confident, and enjoy yourself. Awareness, having a plan, and being alert grows confidence. Be willing to try new things and always plan ahead.

CHAPTER 23

Safety Concerns for Young Adults: Online Dating, Consent, and Campus Life

"Him we proclaim, warning everyone and teaching everyone with all wisdom, that we may present everyone mature in Christ."
Colossians 1:28

Your son or daughter has entered into young adulthood and you can stop worrying—right? You can (and should) stop worrying, but you shouldn't stop educating them. We want our young people to always be maturing and growing in wisdom. By the time your child reaches young adulthood, they feel quite independent and competent. They probably even feel a bit invincible. However the reality is, now they must learn to act and respond like an adult. Yet how can we expect them to do so without having the experience of an adult? We continue to disciple them in discernment and wisdom, while helping them apply it to new life circumstances. We always want to encourage them that if they lack wisdom or understanding, to know that God will provide (James 1:5). Let's continue to look at some common situations.

Dating and Consent

Talking to your young adult about dating relationships outside of high school can be tricky. If you have not fostered relational connection, most young adults feel they are navigating daily life on their own. At this stage, online dating is the avenue many young adults are pursuing in order to meet others. Here is where it is very important to still have influence. You are teaching your young adult to navigate both what dating can and should look like, as well as how to safely get to know someone you meet online.

Kelly was a college student who spent much of her time working and studying, with little social life. After much persuasion from her roommate, she joined a dating app. It offered her flexibility and a perceived sense of safety in getting to know someone from afar. Her routine was to come home late from work, hop online and respond to any connections she had made that day on the dating app.

Isaac was one of them. He was in a college two states away and a sophomore majoring in chemistry. He talked about hiking, his pet cat, had multiple pictures of himself water skiing, hanging out with friends, and even a few pictures with his mom. He listed that he went to church regularly, was studying to become a chemist, and wanted to meet a nice girl. From the outside, all looked perfectly normal, and soon they were chatting back and forth.

Kelli gradually became comfortable with Isaac, she let her guard down and began to share more personal information—where she went to college, what she was studying, where she lives, her phone number, and birthdate, and they began talking about meeting face-to-face. Within several weeks they had a date at a local restaurant that was a state away. They each drove an hour to meet at a place Isaac picked, saying it had good reviews and was right up her alley as far as food choices.

Kelli was excited to meet him and told her roommate how refreshing it was to meet somebody who seemed so normal. She told her roommate the restaurant she would be at and when to expect her home. When she arrived to meet Isaac, they had a lovely dinner and the conversation seemed to go well at first. However, as the meal went on, she began to have some reservations. Something seemed a bit "off," perhaps it was because he was coming on more strongly than she was comfortable with. He was taking her hand, commenting on her appearance often, and making risqué comments.

She caught him eyeing her up and down on several occasions. He also asked probing questions that she couldn't quite put her finger on about her past relationships and experiences dating. Perhaps it was how quickly he became personal or talked about the physical nature of her previous relationships. At one point, she excused herself to the restroom to make a quick call to her roommate. She was feeling a little uncomfortable and needed help coming up with an excuse to end the date earlier than planned.

She returned to the table, finished her meal and she made an excuse for having to get back to her dorm earlier than expected. She politely declined when he asked to go for a walk. When Kelli went to stand up she suddenly felt very wobbly on her feet and lightheaded; she could barely make it to the door, and then realized she may have been drugged. That's the last thing Kelli remembers. She was found several hours later sitting by the side of the road. She had been sexually assaulted by Isaac and left there. Kelly had no idea where she was, no idea where the restaurant or her car was, and she did not have her phone or purse.

Safety Tips for Getting to Know Someone

Young women are more vulnerable to sexual assault than any other population. Most young women know to Google their date they are interested in, but they lack the foresight or wisdom to know what questions to ask and how to safely establish a way to get to know a person.

When on dating sites, somebody can present themselves however they choose. They will present as charming and harmless and down-to-earth. He or she will present themselves in ways that will be attractive and appealing to a vulnerable person, male or female. There are certainly women who take advantage of unsuspecting men, and girls who will use guys for money, fame, or sex. However, more often than not, it tends to be young women who are the most vulnerable.

Regardless, whether it's your son or daughter, help them keep in mind that everyone presents themselves in the best light, and they must use caution in how quickly they trust someone online.

Talk through how long they should wait before they meet in person. What is the important information they should know and how do they confirm the facts to know what's true? Even someone who is googled and presents well, can give a false sense of security. Be aware that *presenting* as transparent and trustworthy is not the same as *being* transparent and trustworthy. Trust must be earned and built, you can only do this by repeatedly watching and observing their behavior in a variety of contexts. Watching them relate to various people in a variety of scenarios is also beneficial.

Look for safe ways to establish getting to know a new person. Getting to know somebody in a group context is beneficial for several reasons. It provides a natural safety when you are not alone. You cannot be easily taken advantage of when others are close by. It also allows a friend to observe and notice things you might miss or were not present to see. Having good friends around allows them to evaluate and give feedback. Pay attention to what your friends and family notice. They may not always be accurate, but they are considering what's best for you. A protective friend will be on the lookout for red flags that you might be tempted to overlook. Take people you trust, and value those who are good at assessing others.

Meet in public places, be willing to take a friend or peer with you, and avoid places that are private. Be wary of going to new or unknown places that you can't verify yourself. Pick a public place you are familiar with. The nice thing about this is you know where all the local restrooms are and what's close by should you need any particular help. Staying close to your home base will create a comfort zone for you and keeps your date on his or her toes.

Meeting in a public place also protects you from inviting someone into your personal world before you know and are confident it is safe. Do not be quick to invite them to where you live or share your daily routines and schedules. It safeguards you against an individual stalking you, showing up unannounced or knowing your where-abouts at all times.

A guy or girl who has access to all your routines and schedules can easily track and spy on your son or daughter without their knowl-edge. Perhaps they're just innocently curious and excited about their relationship, or perhaps they have the makings of a controlling girl-friend or boyfriend. Regardless it is harder to undo information given than to withhold it until trust has been established. Encourage your young adult to be very slow to give information that can't be taken back. Many young people experience stalking, threatening or badger-ing comments, and their lives are disrupted for a season because they were not able to get rid of unwanted attention.

More Practical Suggestions to Share with Young Adults for Online Dating

- Pay attention when things look suspicious. When somebody doesn't have a bio, social media accounts don't match or link, or you're not able to Google them, these are red flags. Avoid these type of profiles.
- Look for ways to confirm a person's identity. Do you have mutual friends? Are they connected with anybody you know? How can you avoid phishing or cat-phishing (a form of online deception using a fake identity to lure people into relationships)? Always block and report anything suspicious. Examples may be: Asking for help financially, pursuing minors or someone who is significantly younger, sending offensive messages to you, attempts to intimidate, threaten, or coerce you; attempts to sell you products or services or pressure you to get involved in a start-up company.
- Look for inconsistencies, whether it is stories they tell, ques-tions about their jobs or former relationships, information about their family or what they do for a living, and a request for your personal information.

- Be slow to share personal information. Especially early on when you have not met, be very careful to avoid personal information like work or home address, your schedule and where you'll be during the day, or usernames or password information.
- When meeting in person it's always helpful to first have multiple conversations and video chats. Meet in a public place where there are many people around and it would be easy to reach out for help. Always let a friend or family member know where you're going, and don't rely on your date for the transportation.
- Some women ask their waiter or waitress before the date shows up to help keep an eye on their food or drink. When they are on a date, it is possible to take the attention away from your food or drink, especially if you were to leave the table, even for a moment.
- Always stick to what makes you the most comfortable, and pay attention to things that feel "off" or "uncomfortable." Be willing to pull out of a situation even if you feel it will be embarrassing or rude. Your safety is always worth a little embarrassment. Then, later you can process it with a trusted friend or family member.
- Look for the opportunity to observe your date's behavior with others: a roommate, their family, how they talk about peers, etc. This reveals a great deal about their character, as well as how they will treat you.

Campus Life

Many young adults look forward to living on campus while at college. This is a great experience for them, whether they decide to go to a small or large campus, a campus situated in a bustling city or out in the middle of the country. How do you help them think through safety skills and wisdom issues for the campus they will be living on? Many young people have a mistaken notion that if they're on campus they are much more protected and safe. This means there may be a false sense of security when it comes to leaving their car doors unlocked, their backpacks and electronics sitting around or their dorm room unlocked. But many crimes, whether it is theft, assault, or crimes of opportunity, do occur on college campuses. As your young person branches out on their own, whether it is in a dorm or in an off-campus apartment, keep teaching them the importance of always practicing good security measures.

Some things to consider:

Does the campus offer security? What does it look like? Are the grounds well-lit at night? Where would you advise a son or daughter to park both to keep their car less vulnerable to break-ins, as well as to stay safe when they walk across campus alone at night?

Likewise, choosing a roommate wisely can make or break a college experience. It is essential to agree upon boundaries with those you live with, including who is and isn't allowed in your living space; whether day or night.

Getting into the practice of letting somebody know where you are is always a helpful way to ensure you will be easier to track down should you be lost, injured, or harmed. For example, if your daughter went to a state park and broke her ankle in the woods, when she didn't return to the dorm, her roommates would be able to tell authorities where to look. If her car breaks down on the side of the road and she's without a phone, somebody can retrace her last steps. It will always be easier to rescue somebody who has checked in with someone on their whereabouts.

Let's say your son is traveling by himself and nobody hears from him for over twenty-four hours. Having information about your child's last known whereabouts always helps police and emergency services to track them down more quickly. Get your young person in the habit of routinely checking in and letting people know where they go. Encourage them that this has nothing to do with you spying on them, but you value their safety. Knowing their whereabouts creates easily traceable steps should something happen to them.

Encouraging your young adult child to take appropriate, wise measures to keep themselves safe is always time well spent. Spending your time worrying about whether they will do everything they can to stay safe is not time well spent. As your child grows in independence, so our faith that the Lord will be watching, guiding, and keeping them must grow as well. It's natural to worry about what is most precious to you—and our children are most precious—but consider again Jesus's counsel that you and your children are more valuable than the birds that God is caring for and that he will care for you and those you love.

CHAPTER 24

God—Our Refuge, Strength, and Very Present Help in Trouble

"God is our refuge and strength,
a very present help in trouble.
Therefore we will not fear though the earth gives way,
though the mountains be moved into the heart of the sea,
though its waters roar and foam,
though the mountains tremble at its swelling. *Selah*
There is a river whose streams make glad the city of God,
the holy habitation of the Most High.
God is in the midst of her; she shall not be moved;
God will help her when morning dawns." Psalm 46:1–5

My hope is that reading this book has given you both biblical principles and practical guidelines that will help to safeguard your child against danger. It is important to remember that although we would all like to believe that we can keep our children completely safe, that is not our guarantee. Our children are moral responders, and they will be facing many of the things mentioned in this book; they will have to make choices to discern what is wise and to do what is right and good. What will you do if you find your child has been victimized or been the one committing the victimization? What will you do when your child caves to temptation, peer pressure, or makes foolish and risky decisions?

As a parent, you will most likely experience a range of emotions: surprise, devastation, grief, anger, maybe even helplessness and despair. You might feel shame that propels you to judge or condemn your child. When your child's actions have heartbreaking repercussions for themselves, you, or the family, you will face a barrage of conflicting emotions and reactions. Be aware of the impact they have on you. You may be tempted to be hopeless or to give up. Perhaps you want to abandon your child or cut them off from you and the rest of your family. Maybe you are overcome with anxiety or fear for the future.

The truth is that, at some point, you are likely to experience the heartbreak and discouragement that comes with loving your children through their temptations, struggles, choices, and suffering. We don't always have a choice in what we will face alongside our children, but we can go to God for the help we need to respond in faith and love. We cannot possibly know all that lies before us and before our children, but we can know who goes with us. Our refuge must always be in God's presence through the hard times. God does not guarantee that we will not face trouble, but he does promise that he will be our refuge and strength in the midst of trouble.

We may grieve, mourn, and struggle with the weight of consequences but we do so with the faith that God is with us in our struggle. He has not abandoned our children, nor us. He specializes in bringing beauty out of ashes, and he is able to do good even in the hardest of situations (Isaiah 61:3).

When you are tempted to despair because of your child's struggles and choices, turn to God's Word and let him interpret your future and your child's future for you. The apostle Paul, in the midst of deep trouble, affirmed this to his fellow Christians:

> We know that God causes all things to work together for good to those who love God, to those who are called according to His purpose . . . What then shall we say to these things? If God is for us, who is against us? He who did not spare His

own son, but delivered him over for us all, how will He not also with Him freely give us all things? Who will bring a charge against God's elect? God is the one who justifies; who is the one who condemns? Christ Jesus is He who died, yes, rather who was raised, and who is at the right hand of God, who also intercedes for us. Who will separate us from the love of Christ? Will tribulation, or distress, or persecution, or famine, or nakedness, or peril, or sword? (Romans 8:28, 31–36 NASB)

Ask the Spirit for Help

It is tempting to forget to turn to the Lord in troubles, or if we do turn to him to demand immediate relief from consequences for our family. But God wants us to turn to him in faith—pouring out our hearts about our troubles and praying impossible prayers. We can pray for the Spirit of God to do what we can't—give the gift of faith to our children and to us. You can be assured that even when you don't know what or how to pray—when all you can do is groan— the Spirit of the living God is within you and will intercede on your behalf (Romans 8:26–27). When we struggle to know what our child needs or how to respond wisely, the Spirit is ready to intercede on our behalf.

God has given us his Spirit as a helper to equip us, and as we ask, the Holy Spirit will give us discernment and guidance in difficult moments. It is the Spirit of God who opens our eyes to perceive what is happening before us and it is the Spirit who gives direction. Have you ever had a subtle nudging that gave you pause or made you check into something your child was doing? We call this many things: a sixth sense, mother's intuition, a gut feeling, or perception and discernment. But we also know that God's Spirit is active and present at all times. When we are struggling to know what to do or are in need of discernment and guidance, God has given us his Spirit who generously works on our behalf.

Cling to Hope

Divine hope is the certainty of God's faithfulness despite what we are going through. It is the certainty that no matter what our children might face, God is up to something good in their lives. Our God is familiar with suffering and well-acquainted with grief (Isaiah 53:3). But the sorrow of the cross was wiped away on Easter morning. Because our God suffered and died for us, we know he understands and sympathizes with our suffering. We know that he forgives our many sins. We know that our children can always turn to God and receive forgiveness and help in their time of need. The resurrection is our guarantee that our hope will not be disappointed.

We can come to the Lord with confidence that he loves our family and treasures our children. Suffering is not a sign that God has abandoned us and our children, instead it is a sign that we are sharing in the sufferings of Christ (Romans 8:7). If we share in his sufferings, we know we will face hard things. But our heartache will produce character, perseverance, and hope that does not disappoint because it rests on God's great love for us and our children (Romans 5:1–5).

Love Wisely

When your children struggle, ask the Spirit for the wisdom to love your child well in the current trouble they are in. Prioritize their welfare and pray and ask others for advice on how to walk wisely alongside them. Your son or daughter needs a parent who can put aside their grief and disappointment and enter into their experience wholeheartedly. Children of all ages need their parents to respond to them with sacrificial love that holds onto them in the face of sin, failure, and brokenness. Look for ways to build bridges with them, extending grace whenever possible, and emulating Christ before then. Your child is both watching and being impacted by what you choose to do with the decisions they've made.

Remember that it is God who will redeem. That eternal perspective gives you the ability to remember what is true, and to tell the difference between what is momentary and what is eternal. It shapes what we do with our heartache and suffering and where our confidence will lie. Parenting our children will consist of a multitude of joys and also heartbreak. Christian homes are not immune from the trials of this world. Hard things happen to believers and unbelievers alike. However, God's promise to us is that he will be our refuge when the world crashes around our family. Godly hope positions us in the center of God's will and reminds us that we live for something better than that which is temporary. It gives us a vision to live for what is eternal so we can trust God with our child's sufferings, as well as our own.

Commit to trust in God at all times—especially in the most disheartening of circumstances. For you know what others mean for evil God intends for good (Genesis 50:20). Believe by faith that he who began a good work, will be faithful to complete it in your child's life (Philippians 1:6).

I opened this book with Psalm 4:8 "In peace I will both lie down and sleep; for you alone, O LORD, make me dwell in safety." In closing, I want to remind you to dwell in the One who is your source of safety and your child's source of safety. He is your refuge and strength and, come what may, will be your refuge and strength. The Lord will be your safeguard and he will be your children's safeguard.

Endnotes

1. Matt Richtel, "'It's Life or Death:' The Mental Health Crisis Among U.S. Teens," *The New York Times*, April 23, 2022, https://www.nytimes.com/2022/04/23/health/mental-health-crisis-teens.html.

2. Sameer Hinduja and Justin W. Patchin, "Cyberbullying: Identification, Prevention, and Response," Cyberbullying Research Center, 2021, https://cyberbullying.org/Cyberbullying-Identification-Prevention-Response-2021.pdf.

3. Kimberly J. Mitchell, Lisa Jones, David Finkelhor, and Janis Wolak, "Trends in Unwanted Sexual Solicitations: Findings from the Youth Internet Safety Studies," *Crimes Against Children Research Center, University of New Hampshire*, February 2014, https://www.unh.edu/ccrc/technologyinternet-victimization.

4. Billy Hallowell, "Prominent Scientist Says 'Religion Will Go Away in a Generation' if Atheists Use This Tactic to Teach Children," *The Blaze*, November 6, 2014, https://www.theblaze.com/news/2014/11/06/prominent-atheist-scientist-cites-slavery-and-gay-marriage-in-this-dire-prediction-religion-will-go-away-in-a-generation.

5. Aleksandr Solzhenitsyn, *The Gulag Archipelago, 1918-1956* (New York: Harper and Row, 1974).

6. Gavin de Becker, *Protecting the Gift: Keeping Children and Teenagers Safe (and Parents Sane)* (New York: Dell Publishing, 2000), 14.

7. CCEF 2015 Regional Conference, "Anxiety: How God Cares for Stressed People, Session 2: 'Practical Steps toward Change.'"

8. "Fast Facts: Preventing Child Sexual Abuse," *Violence Prevention, Centers for Disease Control and Prevention, National for Injury Prevention and Control*, https://www.cdc.gov/violenceprevention/childsexualabuse/fastfact.html.

9. David Finkelhor, Richard Ormrod, Heather Turner, and Sherry Hamby, "The Victimization of Children and Youth: A Comprehensive, National Survey," *Child Maltreatment* 10, no. 1 (February 2005): 5–25, https://doi.org/10.1177/1077559504271287.

10. Anna Slater, *"Predators, Pedophiles, Rapists and Other Sex Offenders: Who They Are, How They Operate, and How We Can Protect Ourselves and Our Children* (Basic Books, 2003).

11. "Fast Facts: Preventing Child Sexual Abuse," *Violence Prevention, Centers for Disease Control and Prevention, National for Injury Prevention and Control,* https://www.cdc.gov/violenceprevention/childsexualabuse/fastfact.html.

12. Gavin de Becker, *Protecting the Gift: Keeping Children and Teenagers Safe (and Parents Sane)* (New York: Random House, 2020), 82–83.

13. Paul Eckman, *Telling Lies: Clues to Deceit in the Marketplace, Politics, and Marriage* (Norton & Company, Incorporated, W.W., 2009), 285.

14. Wiley, "Teaching children in schools about sexual abuse may help them report abuse." Science Daily, April 16 2015, https://www.sciencedaily.com/releases/2015/04/150416083738.htm.

15. "Children and Grooming/Online Predators," *Child Crime Prevention & Safety Center,* 2020, https://childsafety.losangelescriminallawyer.pro/children-and-grooming-online-predators.html.

16. This originally appeared as a CCEF blog article from May 15, 2018, https://www.ccef.org/violence-touches-childs-life/. Used by permission.

17. Admiral Vivek Murthy, *Protecting Youth Mental Health: A U.S. Surgeon General's Advisory* (Office of the Surgeon General, 2021), 3, https://www.hhs.gov/sites/default/files/surgeon-general-youth-mental-health-advisory.pdf.

18. Murthy, *Protecting Youth Mental Health,* 25.

19. Allison Baxter, "How Pornography Harms Children: The Advocate's Role," *Child Law Practice, The American Bar Association,* 2014, https://www.americanbar.org/groups/public_interest/child_law/resources/child_law_practiceonline/child_law_practice/vol-33/may-2014/how-pornography-harms-children--the-advocate-s-role/

20. Baxter, "How Pornography Harms Children"

21. Jasmine Reese, "The Dangers of Vaping and E-Cigarettes," Johns Hopkins Medicine, April 2018, https://www.hopkinsallchildrens.org/ach-news/general-news/the-dangers-of-vaping-and-e-cigarettes.

22. Julie Lowe, *Teens and Suicide: Recognizing the Signs and Sharing the Hope* (Greensboro, North Carolina: New Growth Press, 2020), 9.

23. Lowe, *Teens and Suicide,* 20.